simple
pasta
step-by-step

THUNDER BAY
P·R·E·S·S
San Diego, California

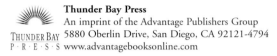

Thunder Bay Press
An imprint of the Advantage Publishers Group
5880 Oberlin Drive, San Diego, CA 92121-4794
www.advantagebooksonline.com

ISBN 1-57145-748-8

Library of Congress Cataloging-in-Publication Data available upon request.

Printed in Korea.

1 2 3 4 5   06 05 04 03 02

ACKNOWLEDGMENTS

Authors: Catherine Atkinson, Juliet Barker, Gina Steer, Vicki Smallwood, Carol Tennant, Mari Mererid Williams, and Elizabeth Wolf-Cohen
Editorial Consultant: Gina Steer
Project Editor: Karen Fitzpatrick
Photography: Colin Bowling, Paul Forrester, and Stephen Brayne
Home Economists and Stylists: Jacqueline Bellefontaine, Mandy Phipps, Vicki Smallwood, and Penny Stephens
Design Team: Helen Courtney, Jennifer Bishop, Lucy Bradbury, and Chris Herbert

All props supplied by Barbara Stewart at Surfaces

NOTE
Recipes using uncooked eggs should be avoided by infants, the elderly, pregnant women, and anyone with a compromised immune system.

Special thanks to everyone involved in this book, particularly Karen Fitzpatrick and Gina Steer.

Contents

STARTERS

FISH & SHELLFISH

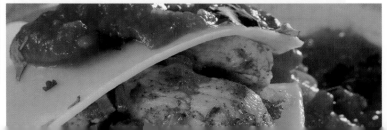

Cleanliness in the Kitchen

It is well worth remembering that many foods can carry some form of bacteria. In most cases, the worst it will lead to is a bout of food poisoning or gastroenteritis, although for certain groups this can be more serious—the risk can be reduced or eliminated by good food hygiene and proper cooking.

Do not buy food that is past its sell-by date and do not consume any food that is past its use-by date. When buying food, use the eyes and nose. If the food looks tired, limp or a bad color or it has a rank, acrid or simply bad smell, do not buy or eat it under any circumstances.

Do take special care when preparing raw meat and fish. A separate cutting board should be used for each; wash the knife, board, and the hands thoroughly before handling any other food.

Regularly clean, defrost, and clear out the refrigerator or freezer—it is worth checking the packaging to see exactly how long it is safe to freeze each product. Avoid handling food if suffering from an upset stomach, as bacteria can be passed through food preparation.

Dishtowels and towels must be washed and changed regularly. Ideally use disposable cloths which should be replaced on a daily basis. More durable cloths should be left to soak in bleach, then washed in the washing machine on a boil wash.

Keep the hands, cooking utensils, and food preparation surfaces clean and do not allow pets to climb onto any work surfaces.

BUYING

Avoid bulk buying where possible, especially fresh produce such as meat, poultry, fish, fruit, and vegetables unless buying for the freezer. Fresh foods lose their nutritional value rapidly, so buying a little at a time minimizes loss of nutrients. It also eliminates a packed refrigerator which reduces the effectiveness of the refrigeration process.

When buying prepackaged goods such as cans or pots of cream and yogurts, check that the packaging is intact and not damaged or pierced at all. Cans should not be dented, pierced, or rusty. Check the sell-by dates even for cans and packages of dry ingredients such as flour and rice. Store fresh foods in the refrigerator as soon as possible—not in the car or the office.

When buying frozen foods, make sure that they are not heavily iced on the outside and the contents feel completely frozen. Ensure that the frozen foods have been stored in the freezer at the correct storage level and the temperature is below 0° F. Pack in cool bags to transport home and place in the freezer as soon as possible after purchase.

PREPARATION

Make sure that all work surfaces and utensils are clean and dry. Hygiene should be given priority at all times. Separate cutting boards should be used for raw and cooked meats, fish, and vegetables. Currently, a variety of good-quality plastic boards come in various designs and colors. This makes differentiating easier and the plastic has the added hygienic advantage of being washable at high temperatures in the dishwasher. If using the board for fish, first wash in cold water, then in hot to prevent odor. Also, remember that knives and utensils should always be thoroughly cleaned after use.

When cooking, be particularly careful to keep cooked and raw food separate to avoid any contamination. It is worth washing all fruits and vegetables regardless of whether they are going to be eaten raw or lightly cooked. This rule should apply even to prewashed herbs and salads.

Do not reheat food more than once. If using a microwave, always check that the food is piping hot all the way through. (In theory, the food should reach 160° F and needs to be cooked at that temperature for at least three minutes to ensure that all bacteria are killed.)

All poultry,must be thoroughly thawed before using. Remove the food to be thawed from the freezer and place in a shallow dish to contain the juices. Leave the food in the refrigerator until it is completely thawed. A 3-lb. whole chicken will take about 26–30 hours to thaw. To speed up the process, immerse the chicken in cold water. However, make sure that the water is changed regularly. When the joints can move freely and no ice crystals remain in the cavity, the bird is completely thawed.

Once thawed, pat the chicken dry. Place the chicken in a shallow dish, cover lightly, and store as close to the base of the refrigerator as possible. The chicken should be cooked as soon as possible.

Some foods can be cooked from

frozen, including many prepacked foods such as soups, sauces, casseroles and breads. Where applicable, follow the manufacturers' instructions.

Vegetables and fruits can also be cooked from frozen, but meats and fish should be thawed first. The only time food can be refrozen is when the food has been thoroughly thawed, then cooked. Once the food has cooled, then it can be frozen again. On such occasions, the food can only be stored for one month.

All poultry and game (except for duck) must be cooked thoroughly. When cooked, the juices will run clear from the thickest part of the bird—the best area to try is usually the thigh. Other meats, like ground meat and pork, should be cooked right the way through. Fish should turn opaque, be firm in texture, and break easily into large flakes.

When cooking leftovers, make sure they are reheated until piping hot and that any sauce or soup reaches the boiling point before eating

STORING, REFRIGERATING, AND FREEZING

Meat, poultry, fish, seafood, and dairy products should all be refrigerated. The temperature of the refrigerator should be between 34–41° F, while the freezer temperature should not rise above 0 °F.

To ensure the optimum refrigerator and freezer temperature, avoid leaving the door open for a long time. Try not to overstock the refrigerator, as this reduces the airflow inside and affects the effectiveness in cooling the food within.

When refrigerating cooked food, allow it to cool down quickly and completely before refrigerating. Hot food will raise the temperature of the refrigerator and possibly affect or spoil other food stored in it.

Food within the refrigerator and freezer should always be covered. Raw and cooked food should be stored in separate parts of the refrigerator. Cooked food should be kept on the top shelves of the refrigerator, while raw meat, poultry, and fish should be placed on bottom shelves to avoid drips and cross-contamination. It is recommended that eggs should be refrigerated in order to maintain their freshness and shelf life.

Take care that frozen foods are not stored in the freezer for too long. Blanched vegetables can be stored for one month; beef, lamb, poultry, and pork for six months; and unblanched vegetables and fruits in syrup for a year. Oily fish and sausages can be stored for three months. Dairy products can last four to six months, while cakes and pastries can be kept for three to six months.

HIGH-RISK FOODS

Certain foods may carry risks to people who are considered vulnerable such as the elderly, the ill, pregnant women, babies, young infants, and those with a compromised immune system.

It is advisable to avoid those foods listed below which belong in a higher-risk category. There is a slight chance that some eggs carry the bacteria salmonella. Cook the eggs until both the yolk and the white are firm to eliminate this risk. Dishes and products incorporating lightly cooked or raw eggs should be eliminated from the diet. Sauces, including hollandaise and mayonnaise, mousses, soufflés, and meringues all use raw or lightly cooked eggs, as do custard-based dishes, ice creams, and sorbets. These are all considered high-risk foods to the vulnerable groups mentioned above.

Certain meats and poultry also carry the potential risk of salmonella and so should be cooked thoroughly until the juices run clear and there is no pinkness left. Unpasteurized products such as milk, cheese (especially soft cheese), pâté, and meat (both raw and cooked) all have the potential risk of listeria and should be avoided.

When buying seafood, buy from a reputable source which has a high turnover to ensure freshness. Fish should have bright, clear eyes, shiny skin, and bright pink or red gills. The fish should feel stiff to the touch, with a slight smell of sea air and iodine. The flesh of fish steaks and fillets should be translucent with no signs of discoloration.

Mollusks, such as scallops, clams, and mussels, are sold fresh and are still alive. Avoid any that are open or do not close when tapped lightly. In the same way, univalves should withdraw back into their shells when lightly prodded. When choosing cephalopods, such as squid and octopus, they should have a firm flesh and pleasant sea smell.

As with all fish, whether shellfish or seafish, care is needed when freezing. It is imperative to check whether the fish has been frozen before. If it has been frozen, then it should not be frozen again under any circumstances.

How To Make Pasta

Homemade pasta has a light, almost silky texture and is very different from the fresh pasta that you can buy vacuum-packed in supermarkets. It is also surprisingly easy to make and little equipment is needed—just a rolling pin and a sharp knife, although if you make pasta regularly it is worth investing in a pasta machine.

MAKING BASIC EGG PASTA DOUGH

Ingredients

2 cups type 001 pasta flour, plus extra for dusting

1 tsp. salt

2 eggs, plus 1 egg yolk

1 tbsp. olive oil

1–3 tsp. cold water

1. Sift the flour and salt into a mound on a clean work surface and make a well in the middle, keeping the sides quite high, so that the egg mixture will not trickle out when added.
2. Beat together the eggs, yolk, oil, and 1 teaspoon of water. Add to the well, then gradually work in the flour, adding extra water if needed, to make a soft but not sticky dough.
3. Knead on a lightly floured surface for 5 minutes, or until the dough is smooth and elastic. Cover with plastic wrap and let rest for 20 minutes at room temperature.

USING A FOOD PROCESSOR

Sift the flour and salt into the bowl of a food processor fitted with a metal blade. Add the eggs, yolk, oil, and water, and pulse-blend until the ingredients are mixed and the dough begins to come together, adding the extra water if needed. Knead for 1–2 minutes, then wrap and rest as before.

ROLLING PASTA BY HAND

1. Unwrap the pasta dough and cut in half. Work with half at a time and keep the other half covered with plastic wrap.
2. Place the dough on a large, clean work surface lightly dusted with flour, then flatten with your hand and start to roll out. Always roll away from you, starting from the center and giving the dough a quarter turn after each rolling. Sprinkle a little more flour over the dough if it starts to get sticky.
3. Continue rolling and turning until the dough is as thin as possible; ideally about ⅛ inch. Make sure that you roll it evenly, or some shapes will cook faster than others.

ROLLING PASTA BY MACHINE

A machine makes smoother, thinner, more consistent pasta than that made by hand-rolling. Most pasta machines work in the same way but you should refer to the manufacturer's directions before using.

1. Clamp the machine securely and attach the handle. Set the rollers at their widest setting and sprinkle lightly with flour. Cut the pasta into four pieces. Cover three of them with plastic wrap and set aside.
2. Flatten the unwrapped pasta dough slightly, then feed it through the rollers. Fold the strip of dough in three, rotate, and feed through the rollers a second time. Continue to roll the pasta this way, narrowing the roller setting by one notch every second time and flouring the rollers if the pasta starts to get sticky. Fold the dough only the first time it goes through each roller width. The dough will get longer and thinner with every rolling—if it gets too difficult to handle, cut the strip in half and work with one piece at a time.
3. If making spaghetti or noodles such

as tagliatelle, the second-to-last setting is generally used. For pasta shapes and filled pastas, the dough should be rolled to the finest setting.
4. Fresh pasta should be dried slightly before cutting. Either drape over a narrow wooden pole for 5 minutes or place on a clean dish towel sprinkled with a little flour for 10 minutes.

You can also buy electric pasta machines that carry out the whole pasta-making process, all you have to do is measure the individual ingredients and add. They can make over 2 lbs. of pasta at a time, but are expensive to buy and take up a lot of space.

SHAPING UP

When cutting and shaping freshly made pasta, have two or three lightly floured dishtowels ready. Arrange the pasta in a single layer, spaced slightly apart, or you may find that they stick together. When they are dry, you can freeze them successfully for up to 6 weeks, by layering in suitable freezer containers between sheets of baking parchment. Spread them out on baking parchment for about 20 minutes, or slightly longer if stuffed, before cooking. When making pasta, do not throw away the trimmings. They can be cut into tiny shapes or thin slivers and used in soups.

Farfalle Use a fluted pasta wheel to cut the pasta sheets into rectangles about 1 x 2 inches. Pinch the long sides of each rectangle in the middle to make a bow. Spread out on a floured dishtowel and leave to dry for at least 15 minutes.

Lasagna This is one of the easiest to make. Simply trim the pasta sheets until neat and cut into lengths the same size as your lasagna dish. Spread the cut sheets on dishtowels sprinkled with a little flour.

Macaroni This is the generic name for hollow pasta. Cut the rolled-out pasta dough into squares, then wrap each around a chopstick, thick skewer, or similar, starting from one of the corners. Slip the pasta off, curve slightly if desired, and leave to dry for at least 15 minutes.

Noodles If using a pasta machine, use the cutter attachment to produce tagliatelle or fettucine, or use a narrower one for tagliarini or spaghetti. To make by hand, sprinkle the rolled-out pasta with flour, then roll up like a jelly roll and cut into thin slices. The thickness of these depends on the noodles required. For linguine, cut into ¼-inch slices and for tagliatelle cut into ⅓-inch slices. Unravel them immediately after cutting. To make thicker ribbon pasta such as pappardelle, use a serrated pastry wheel to cut into wide strips. Leave over a wooden pole for up to 5 minutes to dry out.

Ravioli Cut the rolled-out sheet of dough in half widthwise. Cover one half with plastic wrap to keep it from drying out. Brush the other sheet of dough with beaten egg. Pipe or spoon small mounds—using about 1 teaspoon of filling in even rows, spacing them at 1½ inch intervals. Remove the plastic wrap from the reserved pasta sheet and, using a rolling pin, carefully lift over the dough with the filling. Press down firmly between the pockets of filling to push out any air. Finally, cut into squares with a pastry cutter or sharp knife. Leave on a floured dishtowel for 45 minutes before cooking.

You can also use a ravioli pan (*raviolatore*) to produce perfect even-sized ravioli. A sheet of rolled-out dough is laid over the pan, then pressed into the individual compartments. The filling can then be spooned or piped into the indentations and the second sheet of dough placed on top. To create the individual ravioli squares, a rolling pin is gently rolled over the serrated top. These pans are excellent for making small ravioli containing little amounts of filling.

Three or four simple ingredients combined together make the best fillings. Always season generously with salt and freshly ground black pepper and where the filling is soft, stir in a little beaten egg. Why not try chopped, cooked spinach, ricotta, and freshly grated nutmeg; finely ground turkey, cottage cheese, tarragon, and Parmesan cheese; or white crab meat with mascarpone, finely grated lemon rind, and dill.

Silhouette Pasta If rolled out very thinly, fresh herb leaves can be sandwiched between 2 layers of pasta for a stunning silhouette effect. Put the pasta through a machine set on the very last setting, so that it is paper-thin. Cut in half and lightly brush 1 piece with water. Arrange individual fresh herb leaves at regular intervals over the moistened pasta (you will need soft herbs for this—Italian parsley, basil, and sage are all ideal). Place the second sheet of dry pasta on top and gently press with a rolling pin to seal them together. Sprinkle the pasta with a little flour, then put it through the machine on the second-to-finest setting. Use a pastry wheel, dipped in flour, to cut around the herb leaves to make squares. Leave to dry on a floured dish towel for 20 minutes before cooking.

Tortellini Use a plain cookie cutter to stamp out rounds of pasta about 2 inches in diameter. Lightly brush each with beaten egg, then spoon or pipe about 1 teaspoon of filling into the middle of each round. Fold in half to make a half-moon shape, gently pressing the edges together to seal. Bend the 2 corners around and press together to seal. Leave to dry on a floured dishtowel for 30 minutes before cooking. To make tortelloni, use a slightly larger cutter.

Variations

Flavored pastas are simple and there are dozens of ways that you can change the flavor and color of pasta. You will find that you get a more even color when using a machine, but the speckled appearance of flavored, hand-rolled pasta can be equally attractive.

Chili Add 2 teaspoons of crushed, dried red chilies to the egg mixture before you mix with the flour.

Herbs Stir 3 tablespoons of chopped fresh herbs such as basil, parsley, marjoram, or sage, or 2 tablespoons of finely chopped, strongly flavored herbs like thyme or rosemary into the flour.

Olive Blend 2 tablespoons of black olive paste with the egg mixture, leaving out the water.

Porcini Soak 2 tablespoons dried porcini mushrooms in boiling water for 20 minutes. Drain and squeeze out as much water as possible, then chop very finely. Add to the egg mixture. (Set aside the soaking liquid, strain, and use to flavor the pasta sauce.)

Saffron Sift 1 teaspoon of powdered saffron with the flour.

Spinach Cook ¾ cup prepared spinach in a covered pan with just the water clinging to the leaves, until wilted. Drain and squeeze dry, then chop finely. Add to the egg mixture.

Sun-Dried Tomato Blend 2 tablespoons of sun-dried tomato paste into the egg mixture, leaving out the water.

Whole-Wheat Pasta Substitute half the whole-wheat flour for half of the white flour and add an extra 1–2 teaspoons of water to the mixture.

Pasta Varieties

Pasta has been twisted and curled into an unimaginable number of shapes. There is a vast range of both fresh and dried pasta: short and long, tiny varieties for soup, larger ones for stuffing, and more unusual designer shapes and flavors.

DRIED PASTAS

Buckwheat Pasta Darker in color than whole-wheat pasta, this is made from buckwheat flour. It is gluten-free, so is suitable for people who are intolerant to wheat products. Pizzoccheri are thin, flat noodles twisted into nests and are the most common type of buckwheat pasta.

Corn Pasta Now found on most supermarket shelves, corn pasta is made with cornmeal and the plain variety is a bright yellow color. Like buckwheat pasta, it is gluten-free. When cooking, make sure you use a large pan as it tends to cause the water to foam more than ordinary wheat pasta.

Colored and Flavored Pasta The varieties of these types of pasta are endless. The most popular and easily obtainable are spinach and tomato. Often three colors (white, red, and green) are packed together and labeled "tricolor." Others available in larger food stores and delicatessens include beet, saffron, herb, poppy seed, garlic, chili, mushroom, smoked saffron, and black ink. More unusual types such as blue curaçao liqueur pasta, which has a bright turquoise color, have also been created.

Durum Wheat Pasta This is the most readily available and may be made with or without eggs. Generally, plain wheat pasta is used for long, straight shapes such as spaghetti, whereas pasta containing eggs is slightly more fragile, so is packed into nests or waves. Look for the words "Durum wheat" or "*pasta di semola di grano duro*" on the package when buying, as pastas made from soft wheat tend to become soggy when cooked.

Whole-Wheat Pasta Made with whole-wheat flour, this has a higher fiber content than ordinary pasta, which gives it a slightly chewy texture, nutty flavor, and rich brown color. Whole-wheat pasta takes longer to cook, however, than the refined version. We tend to think of it as a modern product associated with the growth in interest of health foods, but it has been made in northeastern Italy for hundreds of years, where it is known as *bigoli* and is like a thick spaghetti.

PASTA SHAPES
Long Pasta
Spaghetti Probably the best known type of pasta, spaghetti derives its name from the word *spago* meaning "string," which describes its round, thin shape perfectly. Spaghettini is a thinner variety and spaghettoni is thicker. Vermicelli is a very fine type of spaghetti.

Tagliatelle Tagliatelle is the most common type of ribbon-noodle pasta and each ribbon of pasta is usually slightly less than ½ inch wide. It is traditionally from Bologna, where it always accompanies bolognese sauce (rather than spaghetti). It is sold coiled into nests that unravel when cooked. Thinner varieties of tagliarini or tagliolini are also available. A mixture of white and spinach-flavored tagliatelle is

known as *paglia e fieno* which translates as "straw and hay." Fettucine is the Roman version of tagliatelle and is cut slightly thinner.

Ziti Long, thick, and hollow, ziti may be ridged but is usually smooth. It takes its name from *zita*, meaning "fiancée," as it was once traditional to serve it at weddings in southern Italy. Zitoni is a similar larger pasta; mezza zita is thinner.

Short Pasta
There are basically two types of short pasta: *secca* is factory-made from durum wheat and water, which is pressed into assorted shapes and sizes, and *pasta all'uovo* is made with eggs, which is particularly popular in northern Italy, where it is served with meat or creamy sauces. *Pasta all'uovo* is slightly more expensive than plain pasta, but cooks in less time and is less likely to go soggy if overcooked. It is also much more nutritious and has an attractive golden color. There are hundreds of shapes, and some of the most popular are listed below.

Conchiglie As the name implies, these pasta shapes resemble conch shells and are ideal for serving with thinner sauces which will get trapped in the shells. Sizes vary from very tiny ones to large ones which are suitable for stuffing. They may be smooth or ridged conchiglie rigate.

Eliche and Fusilli These are twisted into the shape of a screw, which is where their name comes from. Eliche is often wrongly labeled as "fusilli," as the two are similar, but fusilli is more tightly coiled and opens out slightly during cooking.

Farfalle A popular pasta shape, these are bow- or butterfly-shaped, often with crinkled edges.

Gnocchi Sardi These come from Sardinia and are named after the little gnocchi potato dumplings. Often served with rich meat sauces, they have a somewhat chewy texture.

Macaroni This is known as *maccheroni* in Italy. You may find it labeled as "elbow macaroni" which describes its shape (although it is sometimes almost straight). This was once the most popular imported pasta and is particularly good in baked dishes, notably macaroni and cheese. A thin, quick-cook variety is also available.

Penne Slightly larger, hollow tubes than macaroni, the ends are cut diagonally and are pointed like quills. There are also less well-known varieties including the thinner pennette and even thinner pennini. They are often made with egg or flavored with tomato or spinach.

Pipe This is curved, hollow pasta and is often sold ridged as pipe rigate. The smaller type is known as pipette.

Rigatoni This is substantial, chunky, tubular pasta and is often used for baking. Because the pasta is thick, it tends to be slightly chewier than other short pastas. Rigatoni goes well with meat and strongly flavored sauces.

Rotelle This is thin, wheel-shaped pasta, also known as *ruote* and *trulli* and often sold in packages of two or three colors.

FLAT PASTA

There are many types of long, flat ribbon pastas, but there is only one flat pasta—lasagna—which is usually used for baking in the oven (*al forno*). These thin sheets are layered with a sauce or may be curled into large tubes about 4 inches long to make cannelloni. In Italy, they are usually made from fresh sheets of lasagna rolled around the filling; however, dried tubes are easily available and simple to use.

Three flavors of lasagna are available: plain, spinach, or whole wheat. Most sheets are flat, but some have curled edges which help trap the sauce during cooking and keep it from running to the bottom of the dish. Lasagnette are long, narrow strips of flat pasta and are crimped on one or both long edges. Like lasagna, they are designed to be layered with a sauce and baked.

STUFFED PASTA

Tortellini are the most common of dried pasta shapes and consist of tiny, stuffed pieces of pasta which are folded, and then the ends are joined to make a ring. A specialty of Bologna, larger ones are made from rounds or squares and are joined without leaving a hole in the middle. They are called tortelloni and generally are made with a meat (*alla carne*) or cheese (*ai formaggi*) filling and will keep for up to a year (but always check the sell-by date). Cappelletti, ravioli, and agnalotti are sometimes sold dried, but more often fresh.

SOUP PASTA

Tiny pasta shapes known as *pastina* in Italy come in hundreds of different shapes and are often added to soups. Risi is the smallest type of pasta and looks like grains of rice, whereas orzi, another soup pasta, resembles barley. Slightly larger ones include stellette (stars) and rotelli (wheels). Many are miniature shapes of larger pasta including farfallette (little bows) and conchigliette (little shells).

FRESH PASTA

Fresh pasta has become increasingly popular over the past decade and can be found in the chilled cabinets of supermarkets, as well as being sold loose in specialty stores. Ideally, you should buy fresh pasta on the day you are going to cook it, or use within a day or two. It must be stored in the refrigerator until you are ready to use it, as it contains eggs, which shorten its

keeping time. It generally has a much greater range of stuffed fillings than dried pasta. Ravioli is one of the most common. It is shaped into large squares with fluted edges and is made with many different pasta doughs. The fillings may be anything: for example, spinach and ricotta; mushroom, fish and shellfish; and meat—especially chicken. They may also be shaped into long rectangles, rounds, or ovals.

ASIAN NOODLES

Pasta originated in China and not in Italy, so it is hardly surprising that there is a vast range of Asian noodles available.

Buckwheat Noodles Soba are the most common and are a dark, grayish-brown color. They are featured in Japanese cooking in soups and stir-fries.

Cellophane Noodles Made from mung beans, these are translucent, flavorless noodles and are only available dried. They are never boiled and simply need soaking in very hot water.

Egg Noodles Commonly used in Chinese cooking, they come in several thicknesses, thin and medium being the most popular.

Rice Noodles These are fine, delicate, opaque noodles which are made from rice and are often used in Thai and Malaysian cooking.

Urdon Noodles These are thick Japanese noodles which can be round or flat and are available fresh, dried, or precooked.

Pasta Techniques and Tips

STEPS TO COOKING PERFECT PASTA

Follow a few simple rules to ensure that your pasta is cooked to perfection every time:

1. Choose a big pan. There needs to be plenty of room for the pasta to move around when cooking so that it does not stick together. The best type of pan has a built-in perforated inner pan, so that the pasta can be lifted out of the water and drained as soon as it is done.

2. Cook the pasta in a large quantity of fast-boiling, well-salted water; ideally about 16 cups of water and 1½ to 2 tablespoons of salt for every 12 oz. to 1 lb. of pasta. Some cooks say that the addition of 1–2 teaspoons of olive or sunflower oil not only helps to keep the water from boiling over, but also helps to prevent the pasta from sticking. However, other cooks believe that as long as the pan is large enough and the water is on a full-rolling boil, the pasta will not stick together, nor will the water boil over.

3. Add the pasta all at once, give it a stir, and cover with a lid. Quickly bring back to a rolling boil, then remove the lid—do not cover with a lid during cooking. Once it is boiling, turn down the heat to medium-high and cook the pasta for the required time. It should be al dente which literally translates as "to the tooth" and means that the pasta should be tender, but still firm to the bite. Test frequently toward the end of cooking time; the only way to do this is to take out a piece and try it. Stir the pasta occasionally during cooking with a wooden spoon or fork to make sure that it does not stick to the pan.

4. As soon as the pasta is ready, drain in a colander (or by lifting the draining pan up and out of the water if you have a pasta pot with an inner drainer). Give it a shake, so that any trapped water can drain out. At this stage you can toss the pasta in a little oil or butter if you are not mixing it with a sauce. Set aside a little of the cooking water to stir into the pasta; this not only helps to thin the sauce if needed, but also keeps the cooked pasta from sticking together as it cools.

Some pastas need a little more care than others when cooking. Never stir stuffed pastas vigorously, or they may split open and the filling will be lost in the cooking water. When cooking long, dried pasta such as spaghetti, you will need to coil the pasta into the water as it starts to soften. Hold one end of the strands of spaghetti and push the other to the bottom of the pan, coiling them around, and using a wooden spoon or fork, when the boiling water gets too close to your hand.

An alternative cooking method is to add the pasta to boiling salted water as before, then boil rapidly for 2 minutes. Cover the pan with a tight-fitting lid and turn off the heat. Leave to stand for the full cooking time, then drain and serve in the usual way. Pasta may also be cooked successfully in a microwave, although it does not cook any faster than on the burner. Put the pasta in a large bowl, add salt, then pour over enough boiling water to cover the pasta by at least 1 inch. Microwave on high (100% power) for the times given below. Let the pasta stand for 2–3 minutes before draining.

PASTA COOKING TIMES

Start timing from the moment that the pasta returns to a boil; not from when it was added. Use a kitchen timer if possible, as even a few seconds too long may spoil the pasta.

Fresh 2–3 minutes for thin noodles (although very fine pastas may be ready within seconds of the water returning to a boil), 3–4 minutes for thick noodles and shapes, and 5–7 minutes for filled pastas.

Dried 8–12 minutes; filled pastas can take up to 20 minutes to cook; however, you should always check the package directions, as some pastas labeled "quick cook" only take about 4 minutes.

SERVING QUANTITIES

As an approximate guide, allow 3–4 oz. uncooked pasta per person. Obviously, the amount will depend on whether the pasta is being served for a light or main meal and the type of sauce with which it is being served.

MATCHING PASTA TYPES AND SAUCES

It is entirely up to you which pasta you serve with which sauce, but in general, heavier sauces, with large chunks of meat or vegetables, go with pastas that will trap the sauce and meat in curls and hollows, such as penne, shells, rigatoni, or spirals. On the other hand, soft, fluid sauces suit long pastas such as linguine.

Classic Sauces

Alla Carbonara Pasta with ham, eggs, and cream—the heat of the pasta cooks the eggs to thicken the sauce.

Alla Napoletana Made from fresh tomatoes, olive oil, garlic, and onions.

All'arrabiata A hot sauce with red chilies, tomatoes, and chopped bacon.

All'aglio e Olio Pasta with olive oil and finely chopped garlic.

Alla Marinara A fresh tomato and basil sauce, sometimes with wine, but never seafood.

Con Ragù Meat sauce from Bologna (known as bolognese sauce in English), often made with equal parts ground pork and ground beef. This is often served with tagliatelle, not spaghetti.

SERVING PASTA

In Italy, pasta is usually dressed with the sauce before serving to combine the flavors, but you can top the pasta with the sauce if you prefer, in which case, toss it in a little olive oil or butter to give it an attractive sheen. Cook the sauce and pasta so that they will both be ready at the same time; most sauces can be left to stand for a few minutes and reheated when the pasta is ready. If the pasta is ready before the sauce, drain it and return it to the pan with a tight-fitting lid—it should be fine for a few minutes. Always serve in warmed serving bowls or plates, as pasta loses heat very quickly.

SERVING WINES WITH PASTA

If possible, choose a wine that comes from the same region as the dish you are serving. If there is wine in the sauce, you will be able to serve the rest of the bottle with your meal, so make sure you choose one that you enjoy drinking. Otherwise, pick a wine that matches the strongest flavored ingredient in the sauce. Rich, meaty sauces or highly spiced ones with lots of garlic need a robust, full-bodied wine to go with them. Of course, there is no reason why you should stick to Italian wines, and if you are serving an Asian pasta dish, you may opt for beer or other drinks. Below are ten well-known types of Italian wine.

White Wines

Chardonnay This wine is produced in many parts of the world and is wonderful served with fish dishes. The Italian chardonnay has a faint lemony flavor.

Frascati This wine is made near Rome and is one of the most popular Italian wines. It is crisp and fruity and has quite a lot of body. It goes well with most foods.

Orvieto This wine is named after the town of the same name, just north of Rome. It is dry and soft with a slightly nutty and fruity flavor and is good for summer drinking and serving with fish and white meats.

Soave This wine is one of Italy's most famous wines. The best ones have a distinct hint of almonds and are dry and crisp. It goes well with shellfish, chicken, and light vegetable pasta sauces.

Verdiccho This wine comes in a carved amphora bottle and in Italy is known as *La Lollobrigida*. A crisp, clean, and dry white wine with a slightly metallic edge, it is best when served with fish and seafood.

Red Wines

Barbaresco This wine is full-bodied with an intense flavor and a high tannin content. It teams well with rich pasta dishes, especially beef.

Bardolino This is light and fruity with an almost cherry and slightly bitter almond taste; perfect for duck and game.

Barolo This is one of Italy's finest wines and is a full-bodied red. Serve with rich meaty dishes, game, or spicy sausage pasta sauces.

Chianti This wine is best when young and may be served slightly chilled. Often, it is regarded as the classic accompaniment to pasta.

PASTA EQUIPMENT

When making and cooking pasta, a bare minimum of equipment is needed. Some would say that a rolling pin, a large pan, and a strainer would suffice; however, there are many gadgets that make the process a lot easier.

When Making

Rolling Pin Try to use one that is quite slender and choose a conventional wooden one without handles. In Italy, pasta rolling pins are very long, for rolling out large quantities of pasta at a time, and slightly thicker in the middle with tapering ends.

Pasta Machine A traditional, hand-cranked pasta machine has adjusting rollers and usually cutters for making tagliatelle and finer tagliarini. More complicated ones come with a selection of cutters.

Pasta Wheel This is useful for cutting noodles such as tagliatelle and pappardelle if you do not have a pasta machine, and also for stuffed shapes such as ravioli. This is an inexpensive piece of equipment and less likely to drag or tear the pasta than a knife.

Ravioli Cutter Specially designed, fluted-edged cutters can be bought for cutting pasta. A fluted or plain cookie cutter works just as well.

When Cooking and Serving

Long-handled Pasta Fork This is useful for stirring the pasta to keep the pieces separate during cooking. You can also get wooden pasta hooks which will lift out the strands of pasta so that you can check whether or not it is cooked.

Parmesan Graters These range from simple hand graters to electrical gadgets. If sharp, the fine side of a box grater works equally well.

Parmesan Knife This is used to shave Parmesan off a block. A vegetable peeler may be used as an alternative.

Pasta Cooking Pot Ideally, this should be tall with straight sides and handles and should have an inner basket. When buying, choose one that is not too heavy, and will be easy to manage when full.

Pasta Measurer This is a wooden gadget with several holes for measuring spaghetti. Each hole takes a different amount of pasta for a given number of servings.

Pasta Pantry

INGREDIENTS FOR MAKING EGG PASTA

Only four simple ingredients are needed for basic pasta dough: flour, eggs, olive oil, and salt.

Eggs These should be as fresh as possible and preferably free-range, which tend to have deeper-colored yolks, and, therefore, give the pasta a richer, more golden color. They should be kept at room temperature and not used straight from the refrigerator when making pasta.

Flour The best flour for pasta is Farina Bianca 00 or Type 00 and can be bought from Italian food stores. This type of flour is a very fine wheat flour imported from Italy. You can use strong, white bread flour as an alternative, but the dough will be more difficult to roll out, especially if you are making the pasta by hand.

Olive Oil Strictly speaking, this is not essential for pasta but it gives the dough flavor and makes it slightly softer and therefore easier to roll. Olive oil varies in flavor and color, depending on where it comes from. Generally, those from hotter climates such as southern Italy and Spain have a stronger flavor and darker color than those from areas such as France. Pure or light olive oil is refined to remove any impurities, and is

then blended to give it a light flavor. Virgin olive oil is a pure, first-pressed oil, and extra virgin is a superior product which comes from the first cold pressing of the olives and must have a low acidity; less than 1 percent.

Salt Vital for flavor and should be finely ground, whether regular or sea salt.

INGREDIENTS FOR PASTA SAUCES

Anchovies These are small, silvery fish that grow up to 4 inches long and for centuries have been preserved in salt. They are generally bought as fillets in small cans of around 2 oz. When chopped and mixed with olive oil and garlic, they make an excellent, simple pasta sauce. They are very salty, so remember this when adding seasoning, or if other salty ingredients are being used. Anchovies should be soaked in a little milk or water for about 20 minutes before using.

Capers These are the green flower buds of a bush that grows around the shores of the Mediterranean and they add a sharp piquancy to sauces. Most are sold bottled in vinegar, which makes them particularly good with fish and seafood. If you buy salted capers, rinse them thoroughly, then soak for a few minutes to remove excess salt.

Cheeses Many cheeses are featured in pasta dishes, but you do not have to stick to Italian varieties. However, these naturally go well with Italian-flavored pasta dishes. Gorgonzola is a blue-veined cheese from Lombardy. It melts quickly, so is good in sauces and is also used for stuffing pastas such as ravioli. Mascarpone is a rich, fresh, creamy cheese that melts without curdling. It can be added to pasta with fresh herbs to make a quick sauce. Parmesan

is often grated over pasta dishes or shaved into paper-thin curls when serving. Ricotta is a fresh, soft white cheese that melts beautifully. It has a somewhat bland taste, so is most often combined with other ingredients, such as fresh herbs.

Herbs Both fresh and dried herbs enhance pasta dishes. Those most frequently used are basil, bay leaves, cilantro, dill, oregano and marjoram, parsley, rosemary, and thyme. Basil has a natural affinity with tomatoes and its sweet, fragrant flavor counteracts any acidity. Although basil originated in India, the Italians grow it prolifically. It should be torn or shredded and added at the last moment so that it retains its bright green color and pungent flavor. Dried basil is a poor substitute for fresh—it is better to add a spoonful of green pesto. Look for a recent addition, purple-colored basil, which looks especially attractive when used as a garnish on simple dishes such as pasta tossed in olive oil, garlic, and cheese.

Bay leaves are often used to flavor white sauces and meat dishes such as bolognese. They are always removed before serving, although fresh ones make an attractive garnish. Cilantro is rarely used in Italian pasta dishes, but is often used in Asian noodle dishes. Dill, with its feathery leaves and aniseed flavor, is used a lot in fish and seafood dishes.

Oregano and marjoram are frequently used with tomatoes. Oregano is the wild strain and has a less delicate flavor than marjoram, although the two are interchangeable in dishes.

Recently, curly-leafed parsley has been upstaged by Italian parsley, although either can be used. Rosemary is probably the most pungent herb available and should be used sparingly. Either remove the leaves from the sprig or add the whole sprig to sauces, then remove at the end of cooking and discard.

Thyme is a strongly flavored herb and although it is better when fresh, dried thyme makes a reasonable substitute. It goes well in meat and strongly flavored dishes. Always strip the leaves off the woody stem before chopping.

Mushrooms There are many varieties of fresh, cultivated, and wild mushrooms that feature in pasta sauces. Dried porcini mushrooms are often used for their intense flavor. Only a very small amount is needed; about ⅓ cup is enough for a dish to serve four people. Always soak them first in warm water, then strain the soaking liquid to remove any grit and add to the sauce as well as the mushrooms.

Olives Both black and green olives are used in sauces. Sometimes they are chopped, but more often are used whole (but make sure you pit them first). Buy plain ones in olive oil for adding to sauces; the small shiny ones have the best flavor and should be added at the end of cooking time, or they may become slightly bitter.

Pesto The best pesto is most definitely homemade—there is no substitute. Blend fresh basil leaves with olive oil, pine nuts, and freshly grated Parmesan cheese. Some supermarkets, however, sell fresh pesto in tubs in the refrigerator cases. The bottled varieties

come as green and red (which is made from sun-dried tomatoes and red bell peppers). Pesto adds richness and flavor to sauces or may be used on its own, simply tossed with cooked pasta.

Pine Nuts A vital ingredient of pesto, these small, creamy white nuts have a buttery texture and a hint of pine resin. Buy in small quantities and store in the refrigerator.

Spices Spices are often added to pasta dishes, most notably to those made with Asian noodles. They include chilies, garlic, and saffron. Small red chilies are popular in pasta dishes from southern Italy, but are usually added in small quantities to enhance flavor, rather than to make them hot and fiery. Garlic should be used in small quantities to enhance flavor. The combination of olive oil and garlic forms the basis of many pasta sauces. The longer garlic is cooked, the more mellow the flavor. When buying, look for heads which are firm and showing no signs of sprouting; larger cloves have a sweeter flavor. Saffron is the world's most expensive spice. The stigmas are gathered from the saffron crocus and just a pinch will add a rich, golden color and fragrant flavor to your dish—a little saffron goes a long way.

Tomatoes Many tomato products come from southern Italy where they are ripened on the vine in the hot sun. It is hardly surprising that they feature in so many pasta dishes. The simplest of sauces can be made from canned, peeled plum tomatoes, which come whole or chopped and can now be bought with added flavorings such as chili, basil, and bell peppers. These are excellent when fresh tomatoes are not at their best flavor-wise.

Passata is pulped tomatoes that have been strained to remove the seeds. It comes in cartons and is a useful addition to the pantry. Sun-dried

tomatoes may be plain, dried, or in oil. The dried variety needs rehydrating. This can be done by chopping the sun-dried tomatoes and adding them to a sauce that needs to be cooked for a long time. If you are making a quick sauce, then soften the sun-dried tomatoes by soaking them in hot water for a couple of hours before using. Sun-dried tomatoes in oil already have a soft texture and are excellent for adding a deep, almost roasted flavor to pasta dishes.

Tomato Paste This is a strong, thick paste made from tomatoes, salt, and citric acid. It is sold in tubes and cans— only a little is needed to give your dish a rich, tomato taste. Too much tomato paste can overpower a dish and make it acidic. Sun-dried tomato paste has a sweeter and milder flavor and is a thick mixture of sun-dried tomatoes and olive oil.

Vinegar A dash of red or white wine vinegar may be added to a pasta dish, but the most frequently used in modern cooking is balsamic vinegar (a rich, sweetish, smooth, brown vinegar, aged in wooden barrels until the flavor is very mellow). The best balsamic vinegars are matured for 40 years or more, and are therefore very expensive. Cheaper ones sold in supermarkets have been aged for four to five years and are perfect for adding to sauces.

Fresh Tagliatelle with Zucchini

1 Sift the flour and salt into a large bowl. Make a well in the center and add the eggs and yolk, 1 tablespoon of oil, and 1 teaspoon of water. Gradually mix to form a soft (but not sticky) dough, adding a little more flour or water as necessary. Transfer to a lightly floured surface and knead for 5 minutes or until smooth and elastic. Cover with plastic wrap and let rest at room temperature for about 30 minutes.

2 Divide the dough into 8 pieces. Feed a piece of dough through a pasta machine. Gradually decrease the settings on the rollers, feeding the pasta through each time, until the sheet is very long and thin. If the pasta seems sticky, dust the work surface and both sides of the pasta generously with flour. Cut in half crosswise and hang over a clean pole. Repeat with the remaining dough. Leave to dry for about 5 minutes. Feed each sheet through the tagliatelle cutter, hanging the cut pasta over the pole. Leave to dry for an additional 5 minutes. Wind a handful of pasta strands into nests and leave on a floured dishtowel. Repeat with the remaining dough and leave to dry for 5 minutes.

3 Cook the pasta in plenty of salted boiling water for 2–3 minutes or until al dente.

4 Meanwhile, heat the remaining oil in a large skillet and add the zucchini, garlic, chili, and lemon zest. Cook over a medium heat for 3–4 minutes or until the zucchini is light golden and tender.

5 Drain the pasta, setting aside 2 tablespoons of the cooking water. Add the pasta to the zucchini with the basil and seasoning. Mix well, adding the reserved cooking water. Serve with Parmesan cheese.

INGREDIENTS
Serves 4–6

2 cups bread flour or type 00 pasta flour, plus extra for rolling
1 tsp. salt
2 medium eggs
1 medium egg yolk
3 tbsp. extra virgin olive oil
2 small zucchini, halved lengthwise and thinly sliced
2 garlic cloves, peeled and thinly sliced
large pinch of chili flakes
zest of ½ lemon
1 tbsp. freshly shredded basil
salt and freshly ground black pepper
freshly grated Parmesan cheese, to serve

Helpful Hint

Once made and shaped into nests, the pasta can be stored in an airtight container for 1–2 weeks.

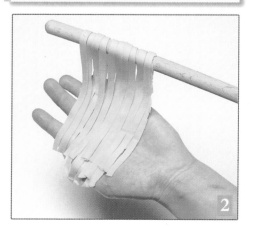

Beet Ravioli with Dill Cream Sauce

1 Make the pasta dough according to the recipe on page 16. Cover with plastic wrap and let rest for 30 minutes.

2 Heat the olive oil in a large skillet. Add the onion and caraway seeds, and cook over a medium heat for 5 minutes or until the onion is softened and lightly golden. Stir in the beets and cook for 5 minutes.

3 Blend the beet mixture in a food processor until smooth, then let cool. Stir in the ricotta, bread crumbs, egg yolk, and Parmesan cheese. Season the filling to taste with salt and pepper and set aside.

4 Divide the pasta dough into 8 pieces. Roll out as for tagliatelle, but do not cut the sheets in half. Lay 1 sheet on a floured surface and place 5 heaping teaspoons of the filling 1 inch apart.

5 Dampen the dough around the heaps of filling and lay a second sheet of pasta over the top. Press around the heaps to seal.

6 Cut into squares using a pastry wheel or sharp knife. Put the filled pasta shapes onto a floured dishtowel.

7 Bring a large pan of lightly salted water to a rolling boil. Drop the ravioli into the boiling water, return to a boil, and cook for 3–4 minutes, until al dente.

8 Meanwhile, heat the walnut oil in a small pan, then add the chopped dill and green peppercorns. Remove from the heat, stir in the crème fraîche, and season well. Drain the cooked pasta thoroughly and toss with the sauce. Spoon onto warmed serving dishes and serve immediately.

INGREDIENTS
Serves 4–6

fresh pasta (see Fresh Tagliatelle with Zucchini, page 16)
1 tbsp. olive oil
1 small onion, peeled and finely chopped
½ tsp. caraway seeds
1 cup chopped cooked beets
6 oz. ricotta cheese
½ cup fresh white bread crumbs
1 medium egg yolk
2 tbsp. grated Parmesan cheese
salt and freshly ground black pepper
4 tbsp. walnut oil
4 tbsp. freshly chopped dill
1 tbsp. green peppercorns, drained and coarsely chopped
6 tbsp. crème fraîche

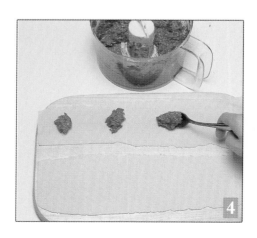

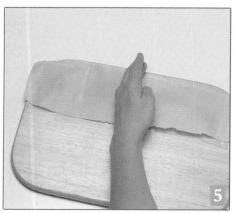

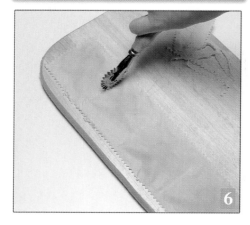

Gnocchi with Broiled Cherry Tomato Sauce

1 Preheat the broiler just before cooking. Bring a large pan of salted water to a boil. Add the potatoes and cook for 20–25 minutes until tender. Drain. Leave until cool enough to handle but still hot, then peel them and place in a large bowl. Mash until smooth, then work in the egg, salt, and enough of the flour to form a soft dough.

2 With floured hands, roll a spoonful of the dough into a small ball. Flatten the ball slightly onto the back of a large fork, then roll it off the fork to make a little ridged dumpling. Place each gnocchi on a floured dishtowel as you work.

3 Place the tomatoes in a flameproof shallow dish. Add the garlic, lemon zest, herbs, and olive oil. Season to taste with salt and pepper, and sprinkle over the sugar. Cook under the preheated broiler for 10 minutes or until the tomatoes are charred and tender, stirring once or twice.

4 Meanwhile, bring a large pan of lightly salted water to a boil, then reduce to a steady simmer. Dropping in 6–8 gnocchi at a time, cook in batches for 3–4 minutes or until they begin bobbing up to the surface. Remove with a slotted spoon and drain well on paper towels before transferring to a warmed serving dish; cover with foil. Toss the cooked gnocchi with the tomato sauce. Serve immediately with a little grated Parmesan cheese.

INGREDIENTS
Serves 4

1 lb. floury potatoes, unpeeled
1 medium egg
1 tsp. salt
about ¾ cup all-purpose flour
1 lb. mixed red and orange cherry tomatoes, halved lengthwise
2 garlic cloves, peeled and finely sliced
zest of ½ lemon, finely grated
1 tbsp. freshly chopped thyme
1 tbsp. freshly chopped basil
2 tbsp. extra virgin olive oil, plus extra for drizzling
salt and freshly ground black pepper
pinch of sugar
freshly grated Parmesan cheese, to serve

Helpful Hint

When cooking the gnocchi, use a very large pan with at least 8 cups of water to give them plenty of room so that they do not stick together.

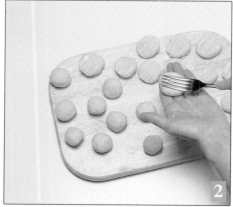

Spinach & Ricotta Gnocchi with Butter & Parmesan

1 Squeeze the excess moisture from the spinach and chop finely. Blend in a food processor with the ricotta cheese, eggs, Parmesan cheese, seasoning, and 1 tablespoon of the basil until smooth. Scrape into a bowl, then add sufficient flour to form a soft, slightly sticky dough.

2 Bring a large pan of salted water to a rolling boil. Transfer the spinach mixture to a pastry bag fitted with a large plain tip. As soon as the water is boiling, pipe 10–12 short lengths of the mixture into the water, using a sharp knife to cut the gnocchi as you go.

3 Bring the water back to a boil and cook the gnocchi for 3–4 minutes or until they begin to rise to the surface. Remove with a slotted spoon, drain on paper towels, and transfer to a warmed serving dish. Cook the gnocchi in batches if necessary.

4 Melt the butter in a small skillet, and when it begins to foam, add the garlic and remaining basil. Remove from the heat and immediately pour over the cooked gnocchi. Season well with salt and pepper and serve immediately with Parmesan cheese shavings.

INGREDIENTS
Serves 2–4

1 cup thawed frozen leaf spinach
8 oz. ricotta cheese
2 small eggs, lightly beaten
½ cup freshly grated Parmesan cheese
salt and freshly ground black pepper
2 tbsp. freshly chopped basil
about ½ cup all-purpose flour
¼ cup unsalted butter
2 garlic cloves, peeled and crushed
Parmesan cheese shavings, to serve

Food Fact

Ricotta is a crumbly, soft white cheese made from whey, a by-product from the manufacture of Pecorino Romano cheese. The curd is compacted so that the cheese can be cut with a knife. It can be eaten by itself, but normally it is used in dishes such as cheesecake.

Tagliatelle with Brown Butter, Asparagus, & Parmesan

1 If using fresh pasta, prepare the dough according to the recipe on page 16. Cut into tagliatelle, wind into nests, and set aside on a floured dishtowel until ready to cook.

2 Bring a pan of lightly salted water to a boil. Add the asparagus and cook for 1 minute. Drain immediately, rinse under cold running water, and drain again. Pat dry and set aside.

3 Melt the butter in a large skillet, then add the garlic and hazelnuts, and cook over a medium heat until the butter turns golden. Immediately

remove from the heat and add the parsley, chives, and asparagus. Leave for 2–3 minutes, until the asparagus is heated through.

4 Meanwhile, bring a large pan of lightly salted water to a rolling boil, then add the pasta nests. Cook until al dente: 2–3 minutes for fresh pasta and according to the package directions for dried pasta. Drain the pasta thoroughly and return to the pan. Add the asparagus mixture and toss together. Season to taste with salt and pepper and spoon into a warmed serving dish. Serve immediately with grated Parmesan cheese.

INGREDIENTS
Serves 6

fresh pasta (see Fresh Tagliatelle with Zucchini, page 16) or 1 lb. dried tagliatelle, such as the white and green variety
12 oz. asparagus, trimmed and cut into short lengths
¾ stick unsalted butter
1 garlic clove, peeled and sliced
¼ cup coarsely chopped, slivered or whole hazelnuts
1 tbsp. freshly chopped parsley
1 tbsp. freshly snipped chives
salt and freshly ground black pepper
½ cup freshly grated Parmesan cheese, to serve

Food Fact

Asparagus is available year-round, but is at its best during May and June. If you buy loose asparagus, rather than prepacked, choose stalks of similar thickness so they will all cook in the same time. It is best to buy asparagus no more than a day before using, but if necessary, you can keep stalks fresh by standing them in a little water.

Pasta with Raw Fennel, Tomato, & Red Onions

1 Trim the fennel and slice thinly. Stack the slices and cut into sticks, then cut crosswise again into fine dice. Deseed the tomatoes and chop them finely. Peel and finely chop or crush the garlic. Peel and finely chop or grate the onion.

2 Stack the basil leaves, then roll up tightly. Slice crosswise into fine shreds. Finely chop the mint.

3 Place the chopped vegetables and herbs in a medium bowl. Add the olive oil and lemon juice, and mix together. Season well with salt and pepper, then leave for 30 minutes to let the flavors develop.

4 Bring a large pan of salted water to a rolling boil. Add the pasta and cook according to the package directions or until al dente.

5 Drain the cooked pasta thoroughly. Transfer to a warmed serving dish, pour over the vegetable mixture, and toss. Serve with the grated Parmesan cheese and extra olive oil to drizzle over.

INGREDIENTS
Serves 6

1 fennel bulb
1½ lbs. tomatoes
1 garlic clove
¼ small red onion
small handful of fresh basil
small handful of fresh mint
7 tbsp. extra virgin olive oil, plus extra to serve
juice of 1 lemon
salt and freshly ground black pepper
4 cups penne or pennette
freshly grated Parmesan cheese, to serve

Food Fact

Fennel is a greenish-white bulbous vegetable that has a distinctive aniseed flavor. It is also known as "Florence fennel" to distinguish it from the herb. When buying fennel, choose a bulb that is well-rounded and as white as possible; the darker green ones may be bitter. Trim off the feathery leaves, chop them finely, and use as a garnish.

Helpful Hint

The vegetables used in this dish are not cooked, but are tossed with the hot pasta. It is important, therefore, that they are chopped finely.

Spaghetti with Fresh Tomatoes, Chili, & Potatoes

1 Preheat the broiler to high 5 minutes before using. Cook the potatoes in plenty of boiling water until tender but firm. Let cool, then peel and cut into cubes.

2 Blend the garlic, basil, and 4 tablespoons of the olive oil in a blender or food processor until the basil is finely chopped, then set aside.

3 Place the tomatoes, basil, and oil mixture in a bowl. Add the chili and season with salt and pepper to taste. Mix together and set the sauce aside.

4 Bring a large pan of salted water to a rolling boil. Add the spaghetti and cook according to the package directions or until al dente.

5 Meanwhile, toss the potato cubes with the remaining olive oil and transfer to a baking tray. Place the potatoes under the preheated broiler until they are crisp and golden, turning once or twice, then drain on paper towels.

6 Drain the pasta thoroughly and transfer to a warmed shallow serving bowl. Add the tomato sauce and the hot potatoes. Toss well and adjust the seasoning to taste. Serve immediately with the grated Parmesan cheese, if desired.

INGREDIENTS
Serves 6

2 medium potatoes, unpeeled

3 garlic cloves, peeled and crushed

small bunch of basil, coarsely chopped

6 tbsp. olive oil

4 large ripe plum tomatoes, skinned, deseeded, and chopped

1 small red chili, deseeded and finely chopped

salt and freshly ground black pepper

1 lb. spaghetti

4 tbsp. freshly grated Parmesan cheese, to serve (optional)

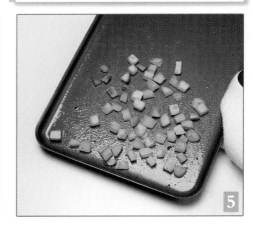

Pasta Genovese with Pesto, Green Beans, & Potatoes

1 Put the basil leaves, garlic, pine nuts, and Parmesan cheese into a food processor and blend until finely chopped. Transfer the mixture to a bowl and stir in the extra virgin olive oil. Season the pesto with salt and pepper and set aside.

2 Bring a pan of salted water to a boil and cook the potatoes for 12–14 minutes or until tender. About 4 minutes before the end of the cooking time, add the beans. Drain and rinse under cold water. Set aside the beans and slice the potatoes thickly or halve them if small.

3 Heat the olive oil in a skillet and add the potatoes. Fry over a medium heat for 5 minutes or until golden. Add the beans and pesto and cook for an additional 2 minutes.

4 Meanwhile, bring a large pan of lightly salted water to a boil. Cook the pasta according to the package directions or until al dente. Drain thoroughly, return to the pan, and add the pesto mixture. Toss well and heat through for 1–2 minutes. Spoon into a warmed serving bowl and serve immediately with Parmesan cheese.

INGREDIENTS
Serves 6

½ cup basil leaves
2 garlic cloves, peeled and crushed
2 tbsp. pine nuts, lightly toasted
¼ cup freshly grated Parmesan cheese
5 tbsp. extra virgin olive oil
salt and freshly ground black pepper
6 oz. new potatoes, scrubbed
4 oz. fine green beans, trimmed
2 tbsp. olive oil
4 cups pasta shapes
extra freshly grated Parmesan cheese, to serve

Tasty Tip

Classic pesto, as used in this recipe, is always made with fresh basil and pine nuts, but other herb variations work equally well. For a change try a cilantro and chili pesto, replacing the basil with fresh cilantro leaves and adding a deseeded and finely chopped red chili; or try an almond and mint pesto, replacing the pine nuts with blanched almonds and the basil with equal amounts of fresh mint and fresh parsley leaves.

Tiny Pasta with Fresh Herb Sauce

1 Bring a large pan of lightly salted water to a rolling boil. Add the pasta and cook according to the package directions or until al dente.

2 Meanwhile, place all the herbs, lemon zest, olive oil, garlic, and chili flakes in a heavy-based pan. Heat gently for 2–3 minutes or until the herbs turn bright green and become very fragrant. Remove from the heat and season to taste with salt and pepper.

3 Drain the pasta thoroughly, setting aside 2–3 tablespoons of the cooking water. Transfer the pasta to a large serving bowl.

4 Pour the heated herb mixture over the pasta and toss together until thoroughly mixed. Check and adjust the seasoning, adding a little of the pasta cooking water if the pasta mixture seems a bit dry. Transfer to warmed serving dishes and serve immediately with grated Parmesan cheese.

INGREDIENTS
Serves 6

3¼ cups tripolini (small bows with rounded ends) or small farfalle
2 tbsp. freshly chopped Italian parsley
2 tbsp. freshly chopped basil
1 tbsp. freshly snipped chives
1 tbsp. freshly chopped chervil
1 tbsp. freshly chopped tarragon
1 tbsp. freshly chopped sage
1 tbsp. freshly chopped oregano
1 tbsp. freshly chopped marjoram
1 tbsp. freshly chopped thyme
1 tbsp. freshly chopped rosemary
finely grated zest of 1 lemon
5 tbsp. extra virgin olive oil
2 garlic cloves, peeled and finely chopped
½ tsp. dried chili flakes
salt and freshly ground black pepper
freshly grated Parmesan cheese, to serve

Helpful Hint

Look for packages of mixed fresh herbs in the supermarket if you do not want to buy individual packages or bunches of all the herbs used in this fresh and vibrant sauce. If you cannot find all the herbs listed, you can increase the quantity of some of them as a substitute for others not being used. Do not add more than 1 tablespoon each of thyme or rosemary though, or their flavor may overpower the sauce.

Louisiana Shrimp & Fettuccine

1 Heat 2 tablespoons of the olive oil in a large pan and add the shrimp shells and heads. Fry over a high heat for 2–3 minutes, until the shells turn pink and are lightly browned. Add half the shallots, half the garlic, half the basil, and the carrot, onion, celery, parsley, and thyme. Season lightly with salt, pepper, and cayenne, and fry for 2–3 minutes, stirring often.

2 Pour in the wine and stir, scraping the pan well. Bring to a boil and simmer for 1 minute, then add the tomatoes. Cook for an additional 3–4 minutes, then pour in ¾ cup of water. Bring to a boil, lower the heat, and simmer for about 30 minutes, stirring often and using a wooden spoon to mash the shrimp shells in order to release as much flavor as possible into the sauce. Lower the heat if the sauce is reducing very quickly.

3 Strain through a sieve, pressing well to extract as much liquid as possible; there should be about 1½ cups. Pour the liquid into a clean pan and bring to a boil, then lower the heat and simmer gently until the liquid is reduced by about half.

4 Heat the remaining olive oil over a high heat in a clean skillet and add the shelled shrimp. Season lightly and add the lemon juice. Cook for 1 minute, lower the heat, and add the remaining shallots and garlic. Cook for 1 minute. Add the sauce and adjust the seasoning.

5 Meanwhile, bring a large pan of lightly salted water to a rolling boil and add the fettuccine. Cook according to the package directions or until al dente, and drain thoroughly. Transfer to a warmed serving dish. Add the sauce and toss well. Garnish with the remaining basil and serve immediately.

INGREDIENTS
Serves 4

4 tbsp. olive oil

1 lb. raw jumbo shrimp, washed and shelled, shells and heads set aside

2 shallots, peeled and finely chopped

4 garlic cloves, peeled and finely chopped

large handful of fresh basil leaves

1 carrot, peeled and finely chopped

1 onion, peeled and finely chopped

1 celery stalk, trimmed and finely chopped

2–3 sprigs fresh parsley

2–3 sprigs fresh thyme

salt and freshly ground black pepper

pinch of cayenne pepper

¾ cup dry white wine

2 cups coarsely chopped, ripe tomatoes

juice of ½ lemon, or to taste

12 oz. fettuccine

Salmon & Roasted Red Bell Pepper Pasta

1 Preheat the broiler to high. Place the salmon in a bowl. Add the shallots, parsley, 3 tablespoons of the olive oil, and the lemon juice. Set aside.

2 Brush the bell pepper quarters with a little olive oil. Cook them under the broiler for 8–10 minutes or until the skins have blackened and the flesh is tender. Place the peppers in a plastic bag until cool enough to handle. When cooled, peel the peppers and cut into strips. Put the strips into a bowl with the basil and the remaining olive oil and set aside.

3 Toast the bread crumbs until dry and lightly browned, then toss with the extra virgin olive oil and set aside.

4 Bring a large pan of salted water to a rolling boil and add the pasta. Cook according to the package directions or until al dente.

5 Meanwhile, transfer the peppers and their marinade to a hot skillet. Add the scallions and cook for 1–2 minutes or until they have just softened. Add the salmon and its marinade and cook for an additional 1–2 minutes or until the salmon is just cooked. Season with salt and pepper.

6 Drain the pasta thoroughly and transfer to a warmed serving bowl. Add the salmon mixture and toss gently. Garnish with the bread crumbs and serve immediately.

INGREDIENTS
Serves 6

8 oz. skinless and boneless salmon fillet, thinly sliced
3 shallots, peeled and finely chopped
1 tbsp. freshly chopped parsley
6 tbsp. olive oil
juice of ½ lemon
2 red bell peppers, deseeded and quartered
handful of fresh basil leaves, shredded
1 cup fresh bread crumbs
4 tbsp. extra virgin olive oil
1 lb. fettuccine or linguine
6 scallions, trimmed and shredded
salt and freshly ground black pepper

Food Fact

Olive oil is graded according to aroma, flavor, color, and acidity—virgin olive oil has less than 2 percent acidity, extra virgin olive oil less than 1 percent.

Spaghettini with Peas, Scallions, & Mint

1 Soak the saffron in 2 tablespoons hot water while you prepare the sauce. Shell the peas if using fresh ones.

2 Melt ½ stick of the butter in a medium skillet. Add the scallions and a little salt, and cook over a low heat for 2–3 minutes or until the scallions are softened. Add the garlic, then the peas and 7 tablespoons water. Bring to a boil and cook for 5–6 minutes or until the peas are just tender. Stir in the mint and keep warm.

3 Blend the remaining butter and the saffron water in a large, warmed serving bowl and set aside.

4 Meanwhile, bring a large pan of lightly salted water to a rolling boil and add the spaghettini. Cook according to the package directions or until al dente.

5 Drain thoroughly, reserving 2–3 tablespoons of the pasta cooking water. Spoon into a warmed serving bowl. Add the pea sauce and toss together gently. Season to taste with salt and pepper. Serve immediately with extra black pepper and grated Parmesan cheese.

INGREDIENTS
Serves 6

pinch of saffron strands
1½ lb. fresh peas or 3 cups frozen petit pois, thawed
¾ stick unsalted butter, softened
6 scallions, trimmed and finely sliced
salt and freshly ground black pepper
1 garlic clove, peeled and finely chopped
2 tbsp. freshly chopped mint
1 tbsp. freshly cut chives
1 lb. spaghettini
freshly grated Parmesan cheese, to serve

Helpful Hint

To develop the full flavor and deep golden color of the saffron, it should be soaked for at least 20 minutes, so do this well before you start cooking. Saffron is one of the few spices that can be kept for several years, but you must store it in an airtight container, away from light.

Fusilli with Tomato & Chorizo Sauce with Roasted Bell Peppers

1 Preheat the broiler to high. Brush the bell pepper quarters with 1 tablespoon of the olive oil, then cook under the preheated broiler, turning once, for 8–10 minutes or until the skins have blackened and the flesh is tender. Place the peppers in a plastic bag until cool enough to handle. When cooled, peel the peppers, slice very thinly, and set aside.

2 Heat the remaining oil in a skillet and add the chorizo. Cook over a medium heat for 3–4 minutes or until starting to brown. Add the garlic and chili flakes, and cook for an additional 2–3 minutes.

3 Add the tomatoes and season lightly with salt and pepper, then cook gently for about 5 minutes or until the tomatoes have broken down. Lower the heat and cook for an additional 10–15 minutes or until the sauce has thickened. Add the peppers and heat gently for 1–2 minutes.

4 Meanwhile, bring a large pan of lightly salted water to a rolling boil. Add the fusilli and cook according to the package directions or until al dente. Drain thoroughly and transfer to a warmed dish. Pour over the sauce, sprinkle with basil, and serve with Parmesan cheese.

INGREDIENTS
Serves 6

1 red bell pepper, deseeded and
   quartered
1 yellow bell pepper, deseeded and
   quartered
4 tbsp. olive oil
¾ cup chorizo, coarsely chopped
   (outer skin removed)
2 garlic cloves, peeled and finely
   chopped
large pinch of chili flakes
3 cups ripe tomatoes, skinned and
   coarsely chopped
salt and freshly ground black
   pepper
4 cups fusilli
basil leaves, to garnish
freshly grated Parmesan cheese, to
   serve

Food Fact

There are two types of chorizo sausage: the dried, salami-type, usually about 2 inches in diameter, and the slightly softer, semidried chorizo, which looks like short fat sausages. The latter type is preferable for this recipe. Both types of chorizo are pork sausages containing chili and paprika, which gives them a vibrant orange-red color.

Pasta with Walnut Sauce

1 Place the toasted walnuts in a blender or food processor with the chopped scallions, one of the garlic cloves, and parsley or basil. Blend to a fairly smooth paste, then gradually add 3 tablespoons of the olive oil until it is well mixed into the paste. Season the walnut paste to taste with salt and pepper, and set aside.

2 Bring a large pan of lightly salted water to a rolling boil. Add the broccoli, return to a boil, and cook for 2 minutes. Remove the broccoli using a slotted spoon, and rinse under cold running water. Drain again and pat dry on paper towels.

3 Bring the water back to a rolling boil. Add the pasta and cook according to the package directions or until al dente.

4 Meanwhile, heat the remaining oil in a skillet. Add the remaining garlic and the chili. Cook gently for 2 minutes or until softened. Add the broccoli and walnut paste. Cook for an additional 3–4 minutes or until heated through.

5 Drain the pasta thoroughly and transfer to a large warmed serving bowl. Pour over the walnut and broccoli sauce. Toss together, adjust the seasoning, and serve immediately.

INGREDIENTS
Serves 4

½ cup walnuts, toasted

3 scallions, trimmed and chopped

2 garlic cloves, peeled and sliced

1 tbsp. freshly chopped parsley or basil

5 tbsp. extra virgin olive oil

salt and freshly ground black pepper

1 lb. broccoli, cut into florets

3 cups pasta shapes

1 red chili, deseeded and finely chopped

Helpful Hint

There is no hard-and-fast rule about which shape of pasta to use with this recipe; it is really a matter of personal preference. Spirali have been used here, but rigatoni, farfalle, garganelle, or pipe rigate would all work well, or you could choose flavored pasta, such as tomato, or a whole-wheat variety for a change.

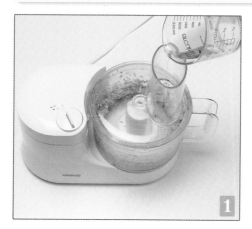

Pasta & Bean Soup

1 Heat the olive oil in a heavy-based pan. Add the celery and prosciutto, and cook gently for 6–8 minutes or until softened. Add the chopped chili and potato cubes and cook for an additional 10 minutes.

2 Add the garlic to the chili and potato mixture, and cook for 1 minute. Add the chopped tomatoes and simmer for 5 minutes. Stir in two thirds of the beans, then pour in the chicken or vegetable stock and bring to a boil.

3 Add the pasta shapes to the soup stock and return it to simmering point. Cook the pasta for about 10 minutes or until al dente.

4 Meanwhile, place the remaining beans in a food processor or blender and blend with enough of the soup stock to make a smooth, thin purée.

5 When the pasta is cooked, stir in the puréed beans with the torn basil. Season the soup to taste with salt and pepper. Ladle into serving bowls. Garnish with shredded basil and serve immediately with plenty of crusty bread.

INGREDIENTS
Serves 4–6

3 tbsp. olive oil
2 celery stalks, trimmed and finely chopped
¾ cup prosciutto or speck, cut in pieces
1 red chili, deseeded and finely chopped
2 large potatoes, peeled and cut into 1 in. cubes
2 garlic cloves, peeled and finely chopped
3 ripe plum tomatoes, skinned and chopped
14-oz. can cranberry beans, drained and rinsed
4 cups chicken or vegetable stock
1 cup pasta shapes
large handful of basil leaves, torn
salt and freshly ground black pepper
shredded basil leaves, to garnish
crusty bread, to serve

Food Fact

Oval cranberry beans have red-streaked, pinkish-brown skin. They have a moist texture and a bittersweet flavor, which makes them excellent in soups. Other canned beans may be used if preferred. Try pinto beans, a smaller, paler version of the cranberry bean, or cannellini beans, which have a soft creamy texture.

Gnocchetti with Broccoli & Bacon Sauce

1 Bring a large pan of salted water to a boil. Add the broccoli florets and cook for about 8–10 minutes or until very soft. Drain thoroughly and leave to cool slightly; then chop finely and set aside.

2 Heat the olive oil in a heavy-based pan. Add the pancetta or bacon and cook over a medium heat for 5 minutes or until golden and crisp. Add the onion and cook for an additional 5 minutes or until soft and lightly golden. Add the garlic and cook for 1 minute.

3 Transfer the chopped broccoli to the bacon or pancetta mixture and pour in the milk. Bring slowly to a boil and simmer rapidly for about 15 minutes or until reduced to a creamy texture.

4 Meanwhile, bring a large pan of lightly salted water to a rolling boil. Add the pasta and cook according to the package directions or until al dente.

5 Drain the pasta thoroughly, setting aside a little of the cooking water. Add the pasta and the Parmesan cheese to the broccoli mixture. Toss, adding enough of the cooking water to make a creamy sauce. Season to taste with salt and pepper. Serve immediately with extra Parmesan cheese.

INGREDIENTS
Serves 6

1 lb. broccoli florets
4 tbsp. olive oil
½ cup finely chopped pancetta or smoked bacon
1 small onion, peeled and finely chopped
3 garlic cloves, peeled and sliced
¾ cup milk
4 cups gnocchetti (little elongated ribbed shells)
½ cup freshly grated Parmesan cheese, plus extra to serve
salt and freshly ground black pepper

Food Fact

Pancetta is an Italian bacon that may be either smoked or unsmoked. You can buy it sliced or in a piece, but it is often sold prepacked, cut into tiny cubes ready for cooking. Thickly cut, smoked bacon makes a good alternative.

Penne with Artichokes, Bacon, & Mushrooms

1 Heat the olive oil in a skillet and add the pancetta or bacon and the onion. Cook over a medium heat for 8–10 minutes or until the bacon is crisp and the onion is just golden. Add the mushrooms and garlic and cook for an additional 5 minutes or until softened.

2 Add the artichoke hearts to the mushroom mixture and cook for 3–4 minutes. Pour in the wine and bring to a boil, then simmer rapidly until the liquid is reduced and syrupy.

3 Pour in the chicken stock and bring to a boil, then simmer rapidly for about 5 minutes or until slightly reduced. Reduce the heat slightly, then slowly stir in the heavy cream and Parmesan cheese. Season the sauce to taste with salt and pepper.

4 Meanwhile, bring a large pan of lightly salted water to a rolling boil. Add the pasta and cook according to the package directions or until al dente.

5 Drain the pasta thoroughly and transfer to a large warmed serving dish. Pour over the sauce and toss together. Garnish with shredded basil and serve with extra Parmesan cheese.

INGREDIENTS
Serves 6

2 tbsp. olive oil

¾ cup chopped smoked bacon or pancetta

1 small onion, peeled and finely sliced

1⅓ cups sliced chestnut mushrooms

2 garlic cloves, peeled and finely chopped

14-oz. can artichoke hearts, drained and halved, or quartered if large

7 tbsp. dry white wine

7 tbsp. chicken stock

3 tbsp. heavy cream

½ cup freshly grated Parmesan cheese, plus extra to serve

salt and freshly ground black pepper

4 cups penne

shredded basil leaves, to garnish

Tasty Tip

Brown-capped chestnut mushrooms are similar in appearance to cultivated button mushrooms, but they have a rich orange-brown color and a slightly stronger, nutty flavor. Tiny, baby chestnut mushrooms are sometimes available and could be used whole or halved in this recipe.

Fettuccine with Wild Mushrooms & Prosciutto

1 Place the dried mushrooms in a small bowl and pour over the hot chicken stock. Leave to soak for 15–20 minutes or until the mushrooms have softened.

2 Meanwhile, heat the olive oil in a large skillet. Add the onion and cook for 5 minutes over a medium heat or until softened. Add the garlic and cook for 1 minute; then add the prosciutto and cook for an additional minute.

3 Drain the dried mushrooms, setting aside the soaking liquid. Coarsely chop and add to the skillet along with the fresh mushrooms. Cook over a high heat for 5 minutes, stirring often or until softened. Strain the mushroom soaking liquid into the pan.

4 Meanwhile, bring a large pan of lightly salted water to a rolling boil. Add the pasta and cook according to the package directions or until al dente.

5 Stir the crème fraîche and parsley seasoning into the mushroom mixture, and heat through gently. Drain the pasta well, transfer to a large warmed serving dish, and pour over the sauce. Serve immediately with grated Parmesan cheese.

INGREDIENTS
Serves 6

½ oz. dried porcini mushrooms
⅔ cup hot chicken stock
2 tbsp. olive oil
1 small onion, peeled and finely chopped
2 garlic cloves, peeled and finely chopped
4 slices prosciutto, chopped or torn
8 oz. mixed wild or cultivated mushrooms, sliced if necessary
1 lb. fettuccine
3 tbsp. crème fraîche
2 tbsp. freshly chopped parsley
salt and freshly ground black pepper
freshly grated Parmesan cheese, to serve (optional)

Food Fact

Prosciutto is produced from pigs fed on whey, a by-product of the local Parmesan cheese industry. The ham is dry-cured, then weighted to flatten it and give it a dense texture. The delicious flavor develops during the year it is left to mature. It is always served in paper-thin slices, either raw or lightly fried.

Tagliarini with Fava Beans, Saffron, & Crème Fraîche

1 If using fresh fava beans, bring a pan of lightly salted water to the boil. Pod the beans and drop them into the boiling water for 1 minute. Drain and rinse under cold water. Drain again. Remove the outer skin of the beans and discard. If using thawed frozen fava beans, remove and discard the skins. Set aside the peeled beans.

2 Heat the olive oil in a saucepan. Add the peeled fava beans and the garlic, and cook gently for 2–3 minutes. Stir in the basil, the crème fraîche, and the pinch of saffron strands, and simmer for 1 minute.

3 Meanwhile, bring a large pan of lightly salted water to a rolling boil. Add the pasta and cook according to the package directions or until al dente. Drain the pasta well and add to the sauce. Toss together and season to taste with salt and pepper.

4 Transfer the pasta and sauce to a warmed serving dish. Sprinkle with chives and serve immediately with Parmesan cheese.

INGREDIENTS
Serves 2–3

8 oz. fresh young fava beans in pods or 1 cup thawed frozen fava beans
1 tbsp. olive oil
1 garlic clove, peeled and chopped
small handful of basil leaves, shredded
about ¾ cup crème fraîche
large pinch of saffron strands
12 oz. tagliarini
salt and freshly ground black pepper
1 tbsp. freshly cut chives
freshly grated Parmesan cheese, to serve

Helpful Hint

If you buy fresh fava beans in their pods (they are available from May to July), look for smooth, plump, bright green pods and use within two days of purchase; they should be cooked the same day as shelling. The skins on the beans become tougher as they age, so if the beans are very young and fresh, there is no need to peel them.

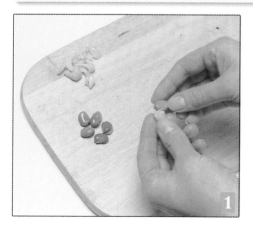

Linguine with Fennel, Crab, & Chervil

1 Bring a large pan of lightly salted water to a rolling boil. Add the pasta and cook according to the package directions or until al dente.

2 Meanwhile, melt the butter in a large pan. Add the carrots, shallots, celery, fennel, and three quarters of the chopped scallions. Cook the vegetables gently for 8–10 minutes or until tender, stirring frequently and taking care that they do not brown.

3 Add the heavy cream and chopped chervil to the vegetable mixture. Scrape the crab meat over the sauce, then stir to mix the sauce ingredients.

4 Season the sauce to taste with salt and pepper and stir in the lemon juice. Drain the pasta thoroughly and transfer to a large warmed serving dish. Pour over the sauce and toss. Garnish with extra chervil, the remaining scallions, and a sprig of dill. Serve immediately.

INGREDIENTS
Serves 6

1 lb. linguine
2 tbsp. butter
2 carrots, peeled and finely diced
2 shallots, peeled and finely diced
2 celery stalks, trimmed and finely diced
1 fennel bulb, trimmed and finely diced
6 scallions, trimmed and finely chopped
1¼ cups heavy cream
3 tbsp. freshly chopped chervil, plus extra for garnish
1 large cooked crab
salt and freshly ground pepper
juice of ½ lemon
sprig of dill, to garnish

Helpful Hint

If you prefer to prepare a cooked crab yourself, start by twisting off the legs and claws, then cracking them open and removing the meat. Next, turn the crab onto its back and twist off the bony, pointed flap. Put the tip of a knife between the main shell and where the legs and claws were attached, twist the blade to lift up and remove, then scrape out the brown meat in the main shell. Pull away and discard the gray, soft gills. Split the body in half and, using a skewer, remove all the white meat from the cavities. An average-sized crab should produce about 8 oz. of white and brown meat.

Farfalle with Smoked Trout in a Dill & Vodka Sauce

1 Bring a large pan of lightly salted water to a rolling boil. Add the pasta and cook according to the package directions or until al dente.

2 Meanwhile, cut the smoked trout into thin slivers, using scissors. Sprinkle lightly with the lemon juice and set aside.

3 Place the cream, mustard, chopped dill, and vodka in a small pan. Season lightly with salt and pepper. Bring the contents of the pan to a boil and simmer gently for 2–3 minutes or until slightly thickened.

4 Drain the cooked pasta thoroughly, then return to the pan. Add the smoked trout to the dill and vodka sauce, then pour over the pasta. Toss gently until the pasta is coated and the trout evenly mixed.

5 Spoon into a warmed serving dish or onto individual plates. Garnish with sprigs of dill and serve immediately.

INGREDIENTS
Serves 4

3½ cups farfalle
5 oz. smoked trout
2 tsp. lemon juice
about ¾ cup heavy cream
2 tsp. whole-grain mustard
2 tbsp. freshly chopped dill
4 tbsp. vodka
salt and freshly ground black pepper
sprigs of dill, to garnish

Food Fact

Two types of smoked trout are available. One resembles smoked salmon in color, texture, and flavor, and can be cut into thin slivers as shown here. Equally delicious is hot smoked rainbow trout, which is available as a whole fish or in fillets. These should be skinned and the bones removed before use. The flesh can then be broken into large flakes. Smoked salmon would also be nice in this recipe.

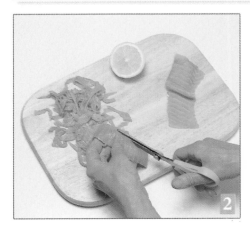

Pappardelle with Smoked Haddock & Blue Cheese Sauce

1 Place the smoked haddock in a pan with 1 bay leaf and pour in the milk. Bring to a boil slowly, cover and simmer for 6–7 minutes or until the fish is opaque. Remove and roughly flake the fish, discarding the skin and any bones. Strain the milk and set aside.

2 Bring a large pan of lightly salted water to a rolling boil. Add the pasta and cook according to the package directions or until al dente.

3 Meanwhile, put the butter, flour, and cream (or milk, if preferred) in a pan and stir to mix. Stir in the reserved warm milk and add the remaining bay leaf. Bring to a boil, whisking all the time until smooth and thick. Gently simmer for 3–4 minutes, stirring frequently. Discard the bay leaf.

4 Add the Dolcelatte or Gorgonzola cheese to the sauce. Heat gently, stirring until melted. Add the flaked haddock and season to taste with nutmeg and salt and pepper.

5 Drain the pasta thoroughly and return to the pan. Add the sauce and toss gently to coat, taking care not to break up the flakes of fish. Spoon into a warmed serving bowl, sprinkle with toasted walnuts and parsley, and serve immediately.

INGREDIENTS
Serves 4

12 oz. smoked haddock
2 bay leaves
1¼ cups milk
14 oz. pappardelle or tagliatelle
2 tbsp. butter
¼ cup all-purpose flour
⅔ cup light cream or extra milk
4 oz. Dolcelatte or Gorgonzola cheese, cut into small pieces
¼ tsp. freshly grated nutmeg
salt and freshly ground black pepper
⅓ cup chopped toasted walnuts
1 tbsp. freshly chopped parsley

Tasty Tip

Dolcelatte is an Italian, semisoft, blue-veined cheese made from cows' milk. It has a smooth creamy texture and a delicate taste. For a more strongly flavored blue cheese sauce, a young Gorgonzola, Roquefort, or blue Stilton can be used instead.

Special Seafood Lasagna

1 Preheat the oven to 400° F. Place the haddock in a pan with the wine, fish stock, onion, and bay leaf. Bring to a boil slowly, cover, and simmer gently for 5 minutes or until the fish is opaque. Remove and flake the fish, discarding any bones. Strain the cooking juices and set aside.

2 Melt ½ stick of the butter in a large saucepan. Add the leeks and garlic, and cook gently for 10 minutes. Remove from the pan using a slotted spoon, and set aside.

3 Melt the remaining butter in a small pan. Stir in the flour, then gradually whisk in the cream, off the heat, followed by the reserved cooking juices. Bring to a boil slowly, whisking until thickened. Stir in the dill and season to taste with salt and pepper.

4 Spoon a little of the sauce into the base of a buttered, shallow, ovenproof dish. Top with a layer of lasagna, followed by the haddock, seafood cocktail, and leeks. Spoon over enough sauce to cover. Continue layering up, finishing with sheets of lasagna topped with sauce.

5 Sprinkle over the grated Gruyère cheese and bake in the preheated oven for 40–45 minutes or until golden brown and bubbling. Serve immediately.

INGREDIENTS
Serves 4–6

1 lb. fresh haddock fillet, skinned
⅔ cup dry white wine
⅔ cup fish stock
½ onion, peeled and thickly sliced
1 bay leaf
¾ stick butter
2 cups trimmed and thickly sliced leeks
1 garlic clove, peeled and crushed
¼ cup all-purpose flour
⅔ cup light cream
2 tbsp. freshly chopped dill
salt and freshly ground black pepper
8–12 sheets dried lasagna verde, cooked
1½ cups ready-cooked seafood cocktail
½ cup grated Gruyère cheese

Helpful Hint

Cook the lasagna in a large pan of boiling salted water with 1 teaspoon olive oil for about 7 minutes, or according to the package directions. Do this even if using pasta labeled pre-cooked. Drain thoroughly and rinse briefly under cold water.

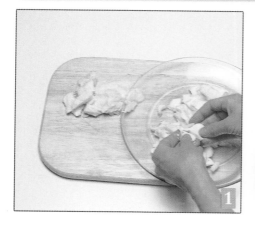

Tuna & Macaroni Timbales

1 Preheat the oven to 350° F. Oil and line the bases of 4 individual timbales or ovenproof molds with nonstick baking parchment and stand in a small roasting pan.

2 Bring a large pan of lightly salted water to a rolling boil. Add the macaroni and cook according to the package directions or until al dente. Drain the cooked pasta thoroughly.

3 Flake the tuna and mix with the macaroni. Divide between the timbales or molds.

4 Pour the light and heavy cream into a small pan. Bring to a boil slowly, remove from the heat, and stir in the Gruyère cheese until melted. Leave to cool for 1–2 minutes, then whisk into the beaten egg and season lightly with salt and pepper. Pour the mixture over the tuna and macaroni and cover each timbale with a small piece of foil.

5 Pour enough hot water into the roasting pan to come halfway up the timbales. Place in the preheated oven and cook for 25 minutes. Remove the timbales from the water and leave to stand for 5 minutes.

6 For the tomato dressing, whisk together the mustard and vinegar in a small bowl, using a fork. Gradually whisk in the sunflower and nut oils, then stir in the chopped tomatoes and the snipped chives.

7 Unmold the timbales onto warmed serving plates and spoon the tomato dressing over the top and around the bottom. Garnish with fresh chives and serve immediately.

INGREDIENTS
Serves 4

1 cup macaroni
7-oz. can tuna in water, drained
⅔ cup light cream
⅔ cup heavy cream
½ cup grated Gruyère cheese
3 medium eggs, lightly beaten
salt and freshly ground black
  pepper
fresh chives, to garnish

FRESH TOMATO DRESSING:

1 tsp. Dijon mustard
1 tsp. red wine vinegar
2 tbsp. sunflower oil
1 tbsp. hazelnut or walnut oil
1¼ cups firm ripe tomatoes,
  skinned, deseeded, and chopped
2 tbsp. freshly snipped chives

Tasty Tip

Other fish can be used to make these pasta timbales. Try a 7-oz. can of white crabmeat, rinsed and drained, or pink salmon with all the bones removed.

Saucy Cod & Pasta Bake

1 Preheat the oven to 400° F. Cut the cod into bite-sized pieces and set aside.

2 Heat the sunflower oil in a large pan. Add the onion and bacon and cook for 7–8 minutes. Add the mushrooms and celery, and cook for 5 minutes or until fairly soft.

3 Add the zucchini and tomatoes to the bacon mixture, and pour in the fish stock or wine. Bring to a boil, then simmer uncovered for 5 minutes or until the sauce has thickened slightly. Remove from the heat and stir in the cod pieces and the tarragon. Season with salt and pepper, then spoon into a large, greased baking dish.

4 Meanwhile, bring a large pan of lightly salted water to a rolling boil. Add the pasta shells and cook according to the package directions or until al dente.

5 For the topping, place the butter and flour in a pan, and pour in the milk. Bring to a boil slowly, whisking until thickened and smooth.

6 Drain the pasta thoroughly and stir into the sauce. Spoon carefully over the fish and vegetables. Place in the preheated oven and bake for 20–25 minutes or until the top is lightly browned and bubbling.

INGREDIENTS
Serves 4

1 lb. cod fillets, skinned
2 tbsp. sunflower oil
1 onion, peeled and chopped
4 slices smoked bacon, rind removed and chopped
1½ cups wiped baby button mushrooms
2 celery stalks, trimmed and thinly sliced
2 small zucchini, halved lengthwise and sliced
14-oz. can chopped tomatoes
7 tbsp. fish stock or dry white wine
1 tbsp. freshly chopped tarragon
salt and freshly ground black pepper

PASTA TOPPING:
2–2½ cups pasta shells
2 tbsp. butter
4 tbsp all-purpose flour
1½ cups milk

Helpful Hint

If you are short of time, you can make a simpler topping. Beat together 2 eggs, 3 tablespoons of plain yogurt, and 3 tablespoons of heavy cream; season to taste with salt and pepper. Add the drained pasta and mix well. Spoon on top of the fish and vegetables, and bake as above for 15–20 minutes or until the top is set and golden brown.

Pasta Provençale

1 Heat the olive oil in a large pan. Add the garlic and onion, and cook gently for 5 minutes. Add the fennel and cook for an additional 5 minutes. Stir in the chopped tomatoes and rosemary sprig. Half-cover the pan and simmer for 10 minutes.

2 Cut the monkfish into bite-sized pieces and sprinkle with the lemon juice. Add to the tomatoes, cover, and simmer gently for 5 minutes or until the fish is opaque.

3 Meanwhile, bring a large pan of lightly salted water to a rolling boil. Add the pasta and cook according to the package directions or until al dente. Drain the pasta thoroughly and return to the saucepan.

4 Remove the rosemary from the tomato sauce. Stir in the black olives, flageolet beans, and chopped oregano, then season to taste with salt and pepper. Add the sauce to the pasta and toss gently together to coat, taking care not to break up the monkfish. Spoon into a warmed serving bowl. Garnish with rosemary and oregano sprigs, and serve immediately.

INGREDIENTS
Serves 4

2 tbsp. olive oil

1 garlic clove, peeled and crushed

1 onion, peeled and finely chopped

1 small fennel bulb, trimmed, halved, and thinly sliced

14-oz. can chopped tomatoes

1 rosemary sprig, plus extra sprig to garnish

12 oz. monkfish, skinned

2 tsp. lemon juice

3½ cups gnocchi pasta

½ cup pitted black olives

7-oz. can flageolet beans, drained and rinsed

1 tbsp. freshly chopped oregano, plus sprig to garnish

salt and freshly ground black pepper

Helpful Hint

Only the tail of the monkfish is eaten and this is usually sold skinned. It has a firm, very white, meaty flesh and a delicious seafood taste, earning it the nickname "poorman's lobster." It may still have a tough transparent membrane covering it, which should be carefully removed before cooking.

Seared Salmon & Lemon Linguine

1 Brush the salmon fillets with the sunflower oil, sprinkle with crushed peppercorns, and press on firmly. Set aside.

2 Bring a large pan of lightly salted water to a rolling boil. Add the linguine and cook according to the package directions or until al dente.

3 Meanwhile, melt the butter in a pan and cook the shredded scallions gently for 2–3 minutes or until soft. Stir in the sour cream and the lemon zest, and remove from the heat.

4 Preheat a griddle or heavy-based skillet until very hot. Add the salmon and sear for 1½–2 minutes on each side. Remove from the pan and leave to cool slightly.

5 Bring the sour cream sauce to a boil, and stir in the Parmesan cheese and lemon juice. Drain the pasta thoroughly and return to the pan. Pour over the sauce and toss gently to coat.

6 Spoon the pasta onto warmed serving plates and top with the salmon fillets. Serve immediately with sprigs of dill and lemon slices.

Helpful Hint

For a less rich and lower-fat version of the sauce, use plain yogurt instead, but do not boil as in step 5. Instead, heat gently with the Parmesan cheese until the cheese melts, then pour over the pasta and toss to coat in the sauce, as above.

INGREDIENTS
Serves 4

4 small skinless salmon fillets, each about 3 oz.
2 tsp. sunflower oil
½ tsp. mixed or black peppercorns, crushed
14 oz. linguine
1 tbsp. unsalted butter
1 bunch scallions, trimmed and shredded
1¼ cups sour cream
zest of 1 lemon, finely grated
½ cup freshly grated Parmesan cheese
1 tbsp. lemon juice
pinch of salt

TO GARNISH:
dill sprigs
lemon slices

Tagliatelle with Tuna & Anchovy Tapenade

1 Bring a large pan of lightly salted water to a rolling boil. Add the tagliatelle and cook according to the package directions or until al dente.

2 Meanwhile, place the tuna, anchovy fillets, olives, and capers in a food processor with the lemon juice and 2 tablespoons of the olive oil, and blend for a few seconds until coarsely chopped.

3 With the motor running, pour in the remaining olive oil in a steady stream; the resulting mixture should be slightly chunky rather than smooth.

4 Spoon the sauce into a bowl. Stir in the chopped parsley and season to taste with black pepper. Check the taste of the sauce and add a little more lemon juice, if needed.

5 Drain the pasta thoroughly. Pour the sauce into the pan and cook over a low heat for 1–2 minutes to warm through.

6 Return the drained pasta to the pan and mix together with the sauce. Spoon into a warmed serving bowl or onto warm individual plates. Garnish with sprigs of Italian parsley and serve immediately.

INGREDIENTS
Serves 4

14 oz. tagliatelle
4-oz. can tuna in oil, drained
2-oz. can anchovy fillets, drained
1¼ cups pitted black olives
2 tbsp. capers in brine, drained
2 tsp. lemon juice
7 tbsp. olive oil
2 tbsp. freshly chopped parsley
freshly ground black pepper
sprigs of Italian parsley, to garnish

Food Fact

Capers are the flower buds of the caper bush, which grows throughout the Mediterranean region. The buds are picked before they open and preserved in vinegar and salt. The word "tapenade" (a mixture of capers, olives, and fish—usually anchovies—pounded to a paste with olive oil) comes from the Provençal word for capers—*tapeno*.

Hot Shrimp Noodles with Sesame Dressing

1 Pour the vegetable stock into a large saucepan and bring to a boil. Add the egg noodles, stir once, then cook according to the package directions, usually about 3 minutes.

2 Meanwhile, heat the sunflower oil in a small skillet. Add the chopped garlic and chili and cook gently for a few seconds. Add the sesame seeds and cook, stirring continuously, for 1 minute or until golden.

3 Add the soy sauce, sesame oil, and shrimp to the skillet. Continue cooking for a few seconds until the mixture starts to bubble, then remove immediately from the heat.

4 Drain the noodles thoroughly and return to the pan. Add the shrimp in the dressing mixture, then the chopped cilantro, and season to taste with black pepper. Toss gently to coat the noodles with the hot dressing.

5 Spoon into a warmed serving bowl or onto individual plates and serve immediately, garnished with sprigs of fresh cilantro.

INGREDIENTS
Serves 4

2½ cups vegetable stock
12 oz. Chinese egg noodles
1 tbsp. sunflower oil
1 garlic clove, peeled and very finely chopped
1 red chili, deseeded and finely chopped
3 tbsp. sesame seeds
3 tbsp. dark soy sauce
2 tbsp. sesame oil
1½ cups shelled cooked shrimp
3 tbsp. freshly chopped cilantro
freshly ground black pepper
fresh cilantro sprigs, to garnish

Food Fact

There are two types of sesame oil that are frequently featured in Asian cooking: the pale and light version, made from untoasted seeds, and the rich dark kind, made from toasted seeds. The latter has a very strong nutty flavor, which can be overpowering in large quantities. If you use the toasted variety in the dressing for this dish, use just 1 tablespoon mixed together with 1 tablespoon of peanut or sunflower oil.

Pan-fried Scallops & Pasta

1 Rinse the scallops and pat dry on paper towels. Place in a bowl and add the olive oil, crushed garlic, and thyme. Cover with plastic wrap and chill in the refrigerator until ready to cook.

2 Bring a large pan of lightly salted water to a rolling boil. Add the penne and cook according to the package directions or until al dente.

3 Meanwhile, make the dressing. Place the sun-dried tomatoes in a small bowl or glass jar and add the vinegars, tomato paste, sugar, salt, and pepper. Whisk well, then pour into a food processor.

4 With the motor running, pour in the sun-dried tomato oil and olive oil in a steady stream to make a thick, smooth dressing.

5 Preheat a large, dry cast-iron griddle pan over a high heat for about 5 minutes. Lower the heat to medium, then add the scallops to the pan. Cook for 1½ minutes on each side. Remove from the pan.

6 Drain the pasta thoroughly and return to the pan. Add the sliced sun-dried tomatoes and dressing, and toss. Divide between individual serving plates. Top each portion with 4 scallops, garnish with fresh thyme or oregano sprigs, and serve immediately.

Handy Hint

Try to buy ready-shelled fresh scallops. If you buy in shells, follow this quick and simple method of opening them. Preheat the oven to 300° F. Place the scallops on a baking sheet, rounded-side down, and put in the oven for about 10 minutes or until the shells just open. When pan-frying the scallops, take care not to overcook them, or they will toughen and lose their moist, tender texture.

INGREDIENTS
Serves 4

16 large scallops, shelled
1 tbsp. olive oil
1 garlic clove, peeled and crushed
1 tsp. freshly chopped thyme
3½ cups penne
4 sun-dried tomatoes in oil, drained and thinly sliced
thyme or oregano sprigs, to garnish

TOMATO DRESSING:

2 sun-dried tomatoes in oil, drained and chopped
1 tbsp. red wine vinegar
2 tsp. balsamic vinegar
1 tsp. sun-dried tomato paste
1 tsp. sugar
salt and freshly ground black pepper
2 tbsp. oil from a jar of sun-dried tomatoes
2 tbsp. olive oil

Smoked Mackerel & Pasta Frittata

1 Preheat the broiler to high just before cooking. Bring a pan of lightly salted water to a rolling boil. Add the pasta and cook according to the package directions or until al dente. Drain thoroughly and set aside.

2 Remove the skin from the mackerel and break the fish into large flakes, discarding any bones, and set aside.

3 Place the eggs, milk, mustard, and parsley in a bowl and whisk together. Season with salt and plenty of freshly ground black pepper, and set aside.

4 Melt the butter in a large, heavy–based skillet. Cook the scallions gently for 3–4 minutes, until soft. Pour in the egg mixture, then add the drained pasta, peas, and half of the mackerel.

5 Gently stir the mixture in the pan for 1–2 minutes or until beginning to set. Stop stirring and cook for about 1 minute until the underneath is golden brown.

6 Spread the remaining mackerel over the frittata, followed by the grated cheese. Place under the preheated broiler for about 1½ minutes or until golden brown and set. Cut into wedges and serve immediately with salad and crusty bread.

INGREDIENTS
Serves 4

¼ cup tricolor pasta spirals or
   shells
8 oz. smoked mackerel
   (or salmon)
6 medium eggs
3 tbsp. milk
2 tsp. whole-grain mustard
2 tbsp. freshly chopped parsley
salt and freshly ground black
   pepper
2 tbsp. unsalted butter
6 scallions, trimmed and
   diagonally sliced
2 oz. frozen peas, thawed
¾ cup grated sharp cheddar cheese

TO SERVE:
green salad
warm crusty bread

Food Fact

A frittata is a thick-set Italian omelette, similar to the Spanish tortilla, which may be served hot or cold, cut into wedges or fingers. To ensure even cooking, it should be cooked very slowly over a low heat and gently stirred only until the mixture starts to set.

Crispy Cod Cannelloni

1 Add 1 teaspoon of the olive oil to a large pan of lightly salted water and bring to a rolling boil. Add the cannelloni tubes and cook uncovered for 5 minutes. Drain and leave in a bowl of cold water.

2 Melt the butter with the remaining oil in a pan. Add the mushrooms and leeks, and cook gently for 5 minutes. Turn up the heat, and cook for 1–2 minutes or until the mixture is fairly dry. Add the cod and cook, stirring, for 2–3 minutes or until the fish is opaque.

3 Add the cream cheese to the pan and stir until melted. Season to taste with salt and pepper, then let the cod mixture cool.

4 Drain the cannelloni. Using a pastry bag without a tip or a spoon, fill the cannelloni with the cod mixture.

5 Mix the Parmesan cheese and bread crumbs together on a plate. Dip the filled cannelloni into the flour, then into the beaten egg, and finally into the bread crumb mixture. Dip the ends twice to ensure they are thoroughly coated. Refrigerate for 30 minutes.

6 Heat the oil for deep frying to 350° F. Fry the stuffed cannelloni in batches for 2–3 minutes or until the coating is crisp and golden brown. Drain on paper towels and serve immediately with fresh herbs or salad leaves.

INGREDIENTS
Serves 4

1 tbsp. olive oil
8 dried cannelloni tubes
2 tbsp. unsalted butter
2½ cups thinly sliced button mushrooms
1 cup trimmed and finely chopped leeks
2 cups skinned and diced cod
¾ cup cream cheese
salt and freshly ground black pepper
2 tbsp. grated Parmesan cheese
1 cup fine fresh white bread crumbs
3 tbsp. all-purpose flour
1 medium egg, lightly beaten
oil for deep-frying
fresh herbs or salad leaves, to serve

Handy Hint

Use a deep, heavy-based pan or a deep-fat fryer for deep-frying. Fill the pan to no more than one-third full with oil. If you do not have a food thermometer to check the oil's temperature, test by dropping in a cube of stale bread; if the oil is hot enough, it will turn golden brown in 40 seconds.

Spaghetti alle Vongole

1 Soak the clams in lightly salted cold water for 8 hours before needed, changing the water once or twice. Scrub the clams, discarding any that have broken shells or that remain open when tapped.

2 Place the prepared clams in a large saucepan and pour in the wine. Cover with a tight-fitting lid and cook over medium heat for 5–6 minutes, shaking the pan occasionally until the shells have opened.

3 Strain the clams and cooking juices through a sieve lined with cheesecloth and set aside. Discard any clams that remain unopened.

4 Heat the olive oil in a pan, and fry the onion and garlic gently for 10 minutes or until very soft.

5 Meanwhile, bring a large pan of lightly salted water to a boil. Add the spaghetti and cook according to the package directions or until al dente.

6 Add the cooked clams to the onions and garlic, and pour in the cooking juices. Bring to a boil, then add the parsley and basil and season to taste with salt and black pepper.

7 Drain the spaghetti thoroughly. Return to the pan and add the clams with their sauce. Toss together gently, then spoon into a large warmed serving bowl or into individual bowls. Serve immediately, sprinkled with oregano leaves.

INGREDIENTS
Serves 4

4 lbs. small fresh clams
6 tbsp. dry white wine
2 tbsp. olive oil
1 small onion, peeled and finely chopped
2 garlic cloves, peeled and crushed
14 oz. spaghetti
2 tbsp. freshly chopped parsley
2 tbsp. freshly chopped or torn basil
salt and freshly ground black pepper
oregano leaves, to garnish

Handy Hint

Cook and eat clams within 24 hours of buying them. Steam them until the shells have just opened, as overcooking will toughen them.

Seafood Pockets with Pappardelle & Cilantro Pesto

1 Preheat the oven to 350° F. To make the pesto, blend the cilantro leaves, garlic, pine nuts, and lemon juice with 1 tablespoon of the olive oil to a smooth paste in a food processor. With the motor running, slowly add the remaining oil. Stir the Parmesan cheese into the pesto, and season to taste with salt and pepper.

2 Bring a pan of lightly salted water to a rolling boil. Add the pasta and cook for 3 minutes only. Drain thoroughly, return to the pan, and spoon over two thirds of the pesto. Toss to coat.

3 Cut out 4 rounds, about 12 inches in diameter, from nonstick baking parchment. Spoon the pasta onto one half of each round. Top each pile of pasta with 2 shrimp, 3 scallops, and a few squid rings. Spoon 1 tablespoon of wine over each serving, then drizzle with the remaining cilantro pesto and top with a slice of lemon.

4 Close the pockets by folding over the other half of the paper to make a semicircle, then turn and twist the edges of the paper to secure.

5 Place the pockets on a baking sheet and bake in the preheated oven for 15 minutes. Serve immediately, letting each person open their own.

INGREDIENTS
Serves 4

11 oz. pappardelle or tagliatelle
8 raw jumbo shrimp, shelled
12 raw bay scallops
8 oz. baby squid, cleaned and cut into rings
4 tbsp. dry white wine
4 thin slices of lemon

CILANTRO PESTO:

1 cup fresh cilantro leaves
1 garlic clove, peeled
¼ cup toasted pine nuts
1 tsp. lemon juice
5 tbsp. olive oil
1 tbsp. grated Parmesan cheese
salt and freshly ground black pepper

Helpful Hint

Prepare whole squid by firmly pulling the pouch and tentacles apart. Remove the transparent quill from the pouch and discard. Rinse the pouch under cold running water, then peel off the dark skin and discard. Slice the pouch and tentacles into rings.

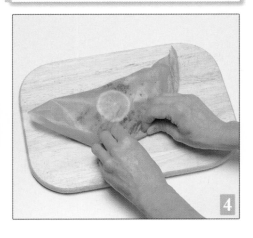

Pasta & Mussels in Tomato & Wine Sauce

1 Scrub the mussels and remove any beards. Discard any that do not close when lightly tapped. Place in a large pan with the bay leaf and pour in the wine. Cover with a tight-fitting lid and steam, shaking the pan occasionally, for 3–4 minutes or until the mussels open. Remove the mussels with a slotted spoon, discarding any that have not opened, and set aside. Strain the cooking liquid through a cheesecloth-lined sieve and set aside.

2 Melt the butter with the oil in a large pan, and gently cook the onion and garlic for 10 minutes until soft. Add the cooking liquid and the tomatoes and simmer uncovered for 6–7 minutes or until soft and the sauce has reduced slightly.

3 Meanwhile, bring a large pan of lightly salted water to a rolling boil. Add the pasta and cook acording to the package directions or until al dente.

4 Drain the pasta thoroughly and return to the pan. Add the mussels, removing the shells if you prefer, with the tomato sauce. Stir in the basil and season to taste with salt and pepper. Toss together gently. Spoon into warmed serving bowls. Garnish with basil leaves and serve with crusty bread.

INGREDIENTS
Serves 4

2 lb. fresh live mussels
1 bay leaf
⅔ cup light red wine
1 tbsp. unsalted butter
1 tbsp. olive oil
1 red onion, peeled and thinly
   sliced
2 garlic cloves, peeled and crushed
1¼ cups ripe tomatoes, skinned,
   deseeded, and chopped
3½ cups fiochetti or penne
3 tbsp. freshly chopped or torn
   basil
salt and freshly ground black
   pepper
basil leaves, to garnish
crusty bread, to serve

Helpful Hint

Some fish sellers still offer mussels by volume
rather than weight: 2¼ pints is the equivalent of 2 pounds.
If you are not cooking mussels within a few hours of
buying them, store in a bowl of water in a cold place or in
the warmest part of the refrigerator on a hot day.
Do not add anything to the water.

Salmon & Spaghetti in a Creamy Egg Sauce

1 Beat the eggs in a bowl with the parsley, dill, half of the Parmesan and pecorino cheeses, and the white wine. Season to taste with freshly ground black pepper and set aside.

2 Bring a large pan of lightly salted water to a rolling boil. Add the spaghetti and cook according to the package directions or until al dente.

3 Meanwhile, cut the salmon into bite-size pieces. Melt the butter in a large skillet with the oil and cook the salmon for 3–4 minutes or until opaque.

4 Drain the spaghetti thoroughly, return to the pan, and immediately add the egg mixture. Remove from the heat and toss well; the eggs will cook in the heat of the spaghetti to make a creamy sauce.

5 Stir in the remaining cheeses and the cooked pieces of salmon, and toss again. Spoon into a warmed serving bowl or onto individual plates. Garnish with sprigs of Italian parsley and serve immediately.

INGREDIENTS
Serves 4

3 medium eggs
1 tbsp. freshly chopped parsley
1 tbsp. freshly chopped dill
⅓ cup freshly grated Parmesan cheese
⅓ cup freshly grated pecorino cheese
2 tbsp. dry white wine
freshly ground black pepper
14 oz. spaghetti
12 oz. salmon fillet, skinned
2 tbsp. butter
1 tsp. olive oil
Italian parsley sprigs, to garnish

Food Fact

This recipe is based on the classic spaghetti alla carbonara, which is made with smoked bacon or pancetta. Here, fresh salmon makes an equally delicious alternative. Make sure that you remove the spaghetti from the heat before adding the egg mixture and keep turning the spaghetti until the eggs cook to a light creamy sauce.

Helpful Hint

You will not need to add salt in this recipe, as the pecorino cheese is very salty.

Creamy Coconut Seafood Pasta

1 Bring a large pan of lightly salted water to a rolling boil. Add the pasta and cook according to the package directions or until al dente.

2 Meanwhile, heat the sunflower and sesame oils together in a saucepan. Add the scallions, garlic, chili, and ginger, and cook for 3–4 minutes or until softened.

3 Blend the coconut milk and cream together in a pitcher. Add the shrimp and crab meat to the pan, and stir over a low heat for a few seconds. Gradually pour in the coconut cream, stirring all the time.

4 Stir the chopped cilantro into the seafood sauce and season to taste with salt and pepper. Continue heating the sauce gently until piping hot, but do not let it boil.

5 Drain the pasta thoroughly and return to the pan. Add the seafood sauce and gently toss together to coat the pasta. Spoon into a warmed serving dish or onto individual plates. Serve immediately, garnished with fresh cilantro sprigs.

INGREDIENTS
Serves 4

14 oz. egg tagliatelle
1 tsp. sunflower oil
1 tsp. sesame oil
4 scallions, trimmed and sliced diagonally
1 garlic clove, peeled and crushed
1 red chili, deseeded and finely chopped
1-in. piece fresh ginger, peeled and grated
⅔ cup coconut milk
7 tbsp. heavy cream
2 cups cooked, shelled jumbo shrimp
1½ cups fresh white crab meat
2 tbsp. freshly chopped cilantro, plus sprigs to garnish
salt and freshly ground black pepper

Helpful Hint

Coconut milk can either be bought in cans or you can make it yourself if you prefer. Put 1 cup natural coconut into a food processor or blender with 1 cup boiling water, and process for 30 seconds. Leave to cool for 5 minutes, then pour into a sieve lined with cheesecloth over a bowl. Leave to drain for a few minutes, then squeeze out as much liquid as possible. Discard the coconut.

Fettuccine with Sardines & Spinach

1 Drain the sardines and cut in half lengthwise. Remove the bones, then cut the fish into 1-inch pieces.

2 Bring a large pan of lightly salted water to a rolling boil. Add the pasta and cook according to the package directions or until al dente.

3 Meanwhile, melt half the butter with the olive oil in a large pan. Add the bread crumbs and fry, stirring until they begin to turn crisp. Add the garlic and pine nuts, and continue to cook until golden brown. Remove from the pan and set aside. Wipe the pan clean.

4 Melt the remaining butter in the pan. Add the mushrooms and cook for 4–5 minutes or until soft. Add the spinach and cook, stirring for 1 minute or until they begin to wilt. Stir in the crème fraîche and lemon zest, and bring to a boil. Simmer gently until the spinach is just cooked. Season the sauce to taste with salt and pepper.

5 Drain the pasta thoroughly and return to the pan. Add the spinach sauce and sardine pieces, and gently toss together. Spoon into a warmed serving dish. Sprinkle with the toasted bread crumbs and pine nuts, and serve immediately.

INGREDIENTS
Serves 4

4-oz. can sardines in olive oil

14 oz. fettuccine or tagliarini

1½ tbsp. butter

2 tbsp. olive oil

1 cup day-old white bread crumbs

1 garlic clove, peeled and finely chopped

½ cup pine nuts

1-1¼ cup chestnut mushrooms, wiped and sliced

1½ cups baby spinach leaves, rinsed

⅔ cup crème fraîche

zest of 1 lemon, finely grated

salt and freshly ground black pepper

Helpful Hint

Choose a full-fat crème fraîche for this recipe rather than half-fat, otherwise it may curdle. Alternatively, use sour cream if you prefer. Other canned fish, such as mackerel fillets, may be substituted for the sardines, but when you buy them, check that they are packed in oil.

Sweet-and-Sour Fish with Crispy Noodles

1 Cut the flounder fillets into 2-inch slices. Mix the flour with the five-spice powder in a bowl. Add the fish, a few pieces at a time, and toss to coat thoroughly. Set aside.

2 Put the ginger, scallions, sherry, soy sauce, sugar, vinegar, and chili sauce in a small pan and season lightly with salt and pepper. Heat gently until the sugar has dissolved, then simmer the sauce for 2–3 minutes.

3 Break the noodles into pieces about 3 inches long. Heat the oil in a deep fryer to

350° F. Deep-fry small handfuls of noodles for about 30 seconds until puffed up and crisp. Remove and drain on paper towels.

4 Deep-fry the flounder for 1-2 minutes or until firm and cooked. Remove and drain on paper towels.

5 Place the cooked fish in a warmed serving bowl. Drizzle the sauce over the fish, and garnish with scallion tassels and slices of red chili. Pile the noodles into another bowl and serve immediately.

INGREDIENTS
Serves 4

12 oz. flounder fillets, skinned

3 tbsp. all-purpose flour

pinch of Chinese five-spice powder

1-in. piece fresh ginger, peeled and grated

4 scallions, trimmed and finely sliced

3 tbsp. dry sherry

1 tbsp. dark soy sauce

2 tsp. soft light brown sugar

1 tsp. rice or sherry vinegar

1 tsp. chili sauce

salt and freshly ground black pepper

4 oz. thin, transparent rice noodles or rice sticks

oil for deep-frying

TO GARNISH:
scallion tassels
slices of red chili

Food Fact

Chinese five-spice powder adds a taste not unlike licorice to this dish. It is made from a mixture of Szechuan pepper, cloves, cassia, fennel, and star anise, ground together to make a golden-brown powder. Add just a tiny pinch, as it has a powerful flavor.

Warm Swordfish Niçoise

1 Place the swordfish steaks in a shallow dish. Mix the lime juice with the oil, and season to taste with salt and pepper. Spoon over the steaks and turn them to coat them evenly. Cover and place in the refrigerator to marinate for 1 hour.

2 Bring a large pan of lightly salted water to a rolling boil. Add the farfalle and cook according to the package directions or until al dente. Add the green beans about 4 minutes before the end of cooking time.

3 Mix the mustard, vinegar, and sugar together in a small jug. Gradually whisk in the olive oil to make a thick dressing.

4 Cook the swordfish in a griddle pan or under a hot preheated broiler for 2 minutes on each side or until just cooked through; overcooking will make it tough and dry. Remove and cut into ¾-inch chunks.

5 Drain the pasta and beans thoroughly and place in a large bowl. Pour over the dressing and toss to coat. Add the cooked swordfish, tomatoes, olives, hard-boiled eggs, and anchovy fillets. Gently toss together, taking care not to break up the eggs.

6 Spoon into a warmed serving bowl or divide the pasta between individual plates. Serve immediately.

INGREDIENTS
Serves 4

4 swordfish steaks, about 1 in. thick, weighing about 6 oz. each

juice of 1 lime

2 tbsp. olive oil

salt and freshly ground black pepper

3½ cups farfalle

1½ cups green beans, trimmed and cut in half

1 tsp. Dijon mustard

2 tsp. white wine vinegar

pinch of sugar

3 tbsp. olive oil

8 oz. ripe tomatoes, quartered

½ cup pitted black olives

2 medium eggs, hard-boiled and quartered

8 anchovy fillets, drained and cut in half lengthwise

Helpful Hint

This dish can also be made with fresh tuna steaks. Prepare and cook in exactly the same way as the swordfish, although tuna can be served slightly rare, if you wish. Do not marinate the fish for more than the time suggested, or it may become overtenderized and lose its firm texture.

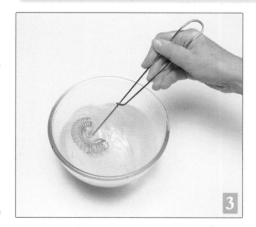

Spaghetti Bolognese

1 Heat the olive oil in a large heavy-based pan. Add the bacon and cook for 5 minutes or until slightly colored. Add the onion, carrot, celery, garlic, and bay leaf, and cook, stirring, for 8 minutes or until the vegetables are soft.

2 Add the ground beef to the pan and cook, stirring with a wooden spoon to break up any lumps in the meat for 5–8 minutes or until browned.

3 Stir the tomatoes and tomato paste into the meat and pour in the wine and stock. Bring to a boil, lower the heat, and simmer for a least 40 minutes, stirring occasionally. The longer you leave the sauce to cook, the more intense the flavor. Season to taste with salt and pepper, and remove the bay leaf.

4 Meanwhile, bring a large pan of lightly salted water to a rolling boil. Add the spaghetti and cook for about 8 minutes or until al dente. Drain and arrange on warmed serving plates. Top with the prepared Bolognese sauce and serve immediately, sprinkled with grated Parmesan cheese.

INGREDIENTS
Serves 4

3 tbsp. olive oil

¼ cup unsmoked bacon, chopped

1 small onion, peeled and finely chopped

1 carrot, peeled and finely chopped

1 celery stalk, trimmed and finely chopped

2 garlic cloves, peeled and crushed

1 bay leaf

5¼ cups ground beef

14-oz. can chopped tomatoes

2 tbsp. tomato paste

⅔ cup red wine

⅔ cup beef stock

salt and freshly gound black pepper

1 lb. spaghetti

freshly grated Parmesan cheese, to serve

Food Fact

Bolognese sauce, or *ragù alla Bolognese*, as it is known in Italy, is enjoyed throughout the world, especially in the United States and Britain. It originated in the city of Bologna in Emilia-Romagna, where it is always served with tagliatelle, rather than spaghetti.

Lasagna

1 Preheat the oven to 400° F. To make the white sauce, melt the butter in a small heavy-based pan. Add the flour and cook gently, stirring, for 2 minutes. Remove from the heat and gradually stir in the milk. Return to the heat and cook, stirring, for 2 minutes or until the sauce thickens. Bring to a boil, remove from the heat, and stir in the mustard. Season to taste with salt, pepper, and nutmeg.

2 Butter a rectangular ovenproof dish and spread a thin layer of the white sauce over the base. Cover completely with 3 sheets of lasagna.

3 Spoon a quarter of the prepared Bolognese sauce over the lasagna. Spoon over a quarter of the remaining white sauce, then sprinkle with a quarter of the grated Parmesan cheese. Repeat the layers, finishing with Parmesan cheese.

4 Bake in the preheated oven for 30 minutes or until golden brown. Garnish with chopped parsley and serve immediately with warm garlic bread.

INGREDIENTS
Serves 4

¾ stick butter

4 tbsp. all-purpose flour

3 cups milk

1 tsp. whole-grain mustard

salt and freshly ground black
  pepper

¼ tsp. freshly grated nutmeg

9 sheets lasagna

1 quantity of prepared Bolognese
  sauce (see page 96)

¾ cup freshly grated Parmesan
  cheese

freshly chopped parsley, to garnish

garlic bread, to serve

Helpful Hint

For a change, use lasagna verdi—this is green lasagna made with spinach. The shape varies according to the manufacturer, and may be flat or wavy. Some have crimped edges, which help to trap the sauce and keep it from running to the bottom of the dish. As sizes differ slightly, it is worth trying several until you find the one that fits your lasagna dish perfectly!

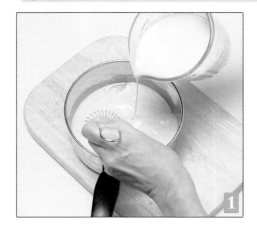

Cannelloni with Spicy Bolognese Filling

1 Preheat the oven to 400° F. To make the Bolognese filling, heat the oil in a large heavy-based pan, add the onion and garlic, and cook for 8 minutes or until soft. Add the ground beef and cook, stirring with a wooden spoon to break up lumps, for 5–8 minutes or until the meat is browned.

2 Stir in the chili flakes, fennel seeds, oregano, tomatoes, and tomato paste. Pour in the wine, and season well with salt and pepper. Bring to a boil, cover, and lower the heat, then simmer for at least 30 minutes, stirring occasionally. Remove the lid and simmer for an additional 10 minutes. Leave to cool slightly.

3 Using a teaspoon, fill the cannelloni tubes with the meat filling. Lay the stuffed cannelloni side-by-side in a lightly greased ovenproof dish.

4 Mix the cream with three-quarters of the Parmesan cheese and the nutmeg. Pour over the cannelloni and sprinkle with the remaining cheese. Bake in the preheated oven for 30 minutes or until golden brown and bubbling. Serve immediately with a green salad.

INGREDIENTS
Serves 6

12 dried cannelloni tubes
1¼ cups heavy cream
¾ cup freshly grated Parmesan cheese
¼ tsp. freshly grated nutmeg
crisp green salad, to serve

SPICY BOLOGNESE FILLING:

2 tbsp. olive oil
1 small onion, peeled and finely chopped
2 garlic cloves, peeled and crushed
5¼ cups ground beef
¼ tsp. crushed chili flakes
1 tsp. fennel seeds
2 tbsp. freshly chopped oregano
14-oz. can chopped tomatoes
1 tbsp. sun-dried tomato paste
⅔ cup red wine
salt and freshly ground black pepper

Helpful Hint

The Bolognese filling can be made with all ground beef, as shown here, or more traditionally with a mixture of half beef and half lean ground pork. Ground chicken or turkey also works well in this recipe, although the color is paler and the flavor less rich, but you can compensate for this by slightly increasing the quantity of herbs and spices.

Spaghetti & Meatballs

1 Preheat the oven to 400° F. Place the chopped tomatoes, tomato paste, chili sauce, and sugar in a pan. Season to taste with salt and pepper, and bring to a boil. Cover and simmer for 15 minutes, then cook uncovered for an additional 10 minutes or until the sauce has reduced and thickened.

2 Meanwhile, make the meatballs. Place the meat, bread crumbs, and onion in a food processor. Blend until all the ingredients are well mixed. Add the beaten egg, tomato paste, parsley, and oregano, and season to taste with salt and pepper. Blend again.

3 Shape the mixture into small balls, about the size of an apricot, and place on a greased baking sheet. Cook in the preheated oven for 25–30 minutes or until browned and cooked.

4 Meanwhile, bring a large pan of lightly salted water to a rolling boil. Add the pasta and cook according to the package directions or until al dente.

5 Drain the pasta and return to the pan. Pour over the tomato sauce and toss gently to coat the spaghetti. Spoon into a warmed serving dish and top with the meatballs. Garnish with chopped parsley and serve immediately with grated cheese.

INGREDIENTS
Serves 4

14-oz. can chopped tomatoes
1 tbsp. tomato paste
1 tsp. chili sauce
¼ tsp. brown sugar
salt and freshly ground black pepper
12 oz. spaghetti
¾ cup grated cheddar cheese, plus extra to serve
freshly chopped parsley, to garnish

FOR THE MEATBALLS:

5 cups ground lean pork or beef
2 cups fresh bread crumbs
1 large onion, peeled and finely chopped
1 medium egg, beaten
1 tbsp. tomato paste
2 tbsp. freshly chopped parsley
1 tbsp. freshly chopped oregano

Tasty Tip

For a crispier outside to the meatballs, you can fry them instead of baking. Heat 2 tablespoons of olive oil in a very large skillet, and cook over a medium heat for about 15 minutes, turning occasionally until well-browned.

Chorizo with Pasta in a Tomato Sauce

1 Melt the butter with the olive oil in a large heavy-based pan. Add the onions and sugar, and cook over a very low heat, stirring occasionally, for 15 minutes or until soft and starting to caramelize.

2 Add the garlic and chorizo to the pan and cook for 5 minutes. Stir in the chili, chopped tomatoes, and tomato paste, and pour in the wine. Season well with salt and pepper. Bring to a boil, cover, reduce the heat, and simmer for 30 minutes, stirring occasionally. Remove the lid and simmer for an additional 10 minutes or until the sauce starts to thicken.

3 Meanwhile, bring a large pan of lightly salted water to a rolling boil. Add the pasta and cook according to the package directions or until al dente.

4 Drain the pasta, setting aside 2 tablespoons of the water, and return to the pan. Add the chorizo sauce with the cooking water, and toss gently until the pasta is evenly covered. Spoon into a warmed serving dish, sprinkle with the parsley, and serve immediately.

INGREDIENTS
Serves 4

2 tbsp. butter
2 tbsp. olive oil
2 large onions, peeled and finely sliced
1 tsp. brown sugar
2 garlic cloves, peeled and crushed
8 oz. chorizo, sliced
1 chili, deseeded and finely sliced
14-oz. can chopped tomatoes
1 tbsp. sun-dried tomato paste
⅔ cup red wine
salt and freshly ground black pepper
4 cups rigatoni
freshly chopped parsley, to garnish

Helpful Hint

Although there are many different types of chili, they all have a hot, spicy flavor. Take care when preparing chilies, as the volatile oils in the seeds and the membrane can cause irritation—wash your hands thoroughly afterward.

Moroccan Penne

1 Preheat the oven to 400° F. Heat the sunflower oil in a large flameproof casserole dish. Add the chopped onion and fry for 5 minutes or until softened.

2 Using a mortar and pestle, pound the garlic, coriander seeds, cumin seeds, and grated nutmeg together into a paste. Add to the onion and cook for 3 minutes.

3 Add the ground lamb to the casserole and fry, stirring with a wooden spoon for 4–5 minutes or until the meat has broken up and browned.

4 Add the eggplant to the meat and fry for 5 minutes. Stir in the chopped tomatoes and vegetable stock, and bring to a boil. Add the apricots and olives, then season well with salt and pepper. Return to a boil, lower the heat, and simmer for 15 minutes.

5 Add the penne to the casserole, stir well, then cover and place in the preheated oven. Cook for 10 minutes, then stir and return to the oven uncovered for an additional 15–20 minutes or until the pasta is al dente. Remove from the oven, sprinkle with toasted pine nuts, and serve immediately.

INGREDIENTS
Serves 4

1 tbsp. sunflower oil
1 red onion, peeled and chopped
2 garlic cloves, peeled and crushed
1 tbsp. coriander seeds
¼ tsp. cumin seeds
¼ tsp. freshly grated nutmeg
5 cups ground lean lamb
1 eggplant, trimmed and diced
14-oz. can chopped tomatoes
1¼ cups vegetable stock
½ cup chopped dried apricots
12 black olives, pitted
salt and freshly ground black pepper
3 cups penne
1 tbsp. toasted pine nuts, to garnish

Helpful Hint

You can sometimes buy toasted pine nuts, but if you cannot find any, they are easy to toast. Sprinkle them on a foil-lined broiler pan and place under a medium broiler for 3–4 minutes, turning frequently until they are golden brown. Alternatively, fry them in a nonstick skillet, tossing the nuts every few seconds. Always watch nuts when cooking, as they can burn easily.

Spicy Chili Beef

1 Heat the olive oil in a large heavy-based pan. Add the onion and red bell pepper, and cook for 5 minutes or until beginning to soften. Add the ground beef and cook over a high heat for 5–8 minutes or until the meat is browned. Stir with a wooden spoon during cooking to break up any lumps in the meat. Add the garlic and chilies, fry for 1 minute, then season to taste.

2 Add the chopped tomatoes, tomato paste, and the kidney beans to the pan. Bring to a boil, lower the heat, and simmer covered for at least 40 minutes, stirring occasionally. Stir in the grated chocolate and cook for 3 minutes or until melted.

3 Meanwhile, bring a large pan of lightly salted water to a rolling boil. Add the fusilli and cook according to the package directions or until al dente.

4 Drain the pasta, return to the pan, and toss with the butter and parsley. Spoon into a warmed serving dish or spoon onto individual plates. Spoon the sauce over the pasta. Sprinkle with paprika and serve immediately with spoonfuls of sour cream.

INGREDIENTS
Serves 4

2 tbsp. olive oil

1 onion, peeled and finely chopped

1 red bell pepper, deseeded and sliced

5 cups ground beef

2 garlic cloves, peeled and crushed

2 red chilies, deseeded and finely sliced

salt and freshly ground black pepper

14-oz. can chopped tomatoes

2 tbsp. tomato paste

14-oz. can red kidney beans, drained

2 squares good-quality dark chocolate, grated

3 cups dried fusilli

1 tsp. butter

2 tbsp. freshly chopped Italian parsley

paprika, to garnish

sour cream, to serve

Food Fact

The chocolate in this traditional spicy Mexican dish adds rich warm undertones, color, and a slight sweetness, but no one will realize it is there unless you tell them. For maximum flavor, use a good quality, dark chocolate with a low sugar content and a high percentage of cocoa solids.

Pasta & Pork Ragù

1 Heat the sunflower oil in a large skillet. Add the sliced leek and cook, stirring frequently, for 5 minutes or until softened. Add the pork and cook, stirring, for 4 minutes or until sealed.

2 Add the crushed garlic and the paprika and cayenne peppers to the pan. Stir until all the pork is lightly coated in the garlic and pepper mixture.

3 Pour in the wine and 1¾ cups of the vegetable stock. Add the cranberry beans and carrots, and season to taste with salt and pepper. Bring the sauce to a boil, then lower the heat and simmer for 5 minutes.

4 Meanwhile, place the egg tagliatelle in a large saucepan of lightly salted boiling water, cover and simmer for 5 minutes or until the pasta is cooked al dente.

5 Drain the pasta, then add to the pork ragù; toss well. Adjust the seasoning, then spoon into a warmed serving dish. Sprinkle with chopped parsley and serve with a little crème fraîche.

INGREDIENTS
Serves 4

1 tbsp. sunflower oil
1 leek, trimmed and thinly sliced
2½ cups diced pork tenderloin
1 garlic clove, peeled and crushed
2 tsp. paprika
¼ tsp. cayenne pepper
⅔ cup white wine
2½ cups vegetable stock
14-oz. can cranberry beans, drained and rinsed
2 carrots, peeled and diced
salt and freshly ground black pepper
8 oz. fresh egg tagliatelle
1 tbsp. freshly chopped parsley, to garnish
crème fraîche, to serve

Helpful Hint

Pork tenderloin, also known as "fillet," is a very lean and tender cut of pork. It needs little cooking time, so is perfect for this quick and simple dish. Sirloin steak or boneless skinned chicken breast, cut into thin strips, could be used instead, if preferred.

Sausage & Red Currant Pasta Bake

1 Preheat the oven to 425° F. Prick the sausages, place in a shallow ovenproof dish, and toss in the sunflower oil. Cook in the oven for 25–30 minutes or until golden brown.

2 Meanwhile, melt the butter in a skillet. Add the sliced onion and fry for 5 minutes or until golden brown. Stir in the flour and cook for 2 minutes. Remove the pan from the heat and gradually stir in the chicken stock with the port or red wine.

3 Return the pan to the heat and bring to a boil, stirring continuously until the sauce starts to thicken. Add the thyme, bay leaf, and red currant jelly, and season well with salt and pepper. Simmer the sauce for 5 minutes.

4 Bring a large pan of salted water to a rolling boil. Add the pasta and cook for about 4 minutes or until al dente. Drain thoroughly and set aside.

5 Lower the oven temperature to 400° F. Remove the sausages from the oven, drain off any excess fat, and return the sausages to the dish. Add the pasta. Pour over the sauce, discarding the bay leaf, and toss together. Sprinkle with the Gruyère cheese and return to the oven for 15–20 minutes or until bubbling and golden brown. Serve immediately, garnished with thyme sprigs.

INGREDIENTS
Serves 4

1 lb. good-quality, thick pork sausages
2 tsp. sunflower oil
2 tbsp. butter
1 onion, peeled and sliced
2 tbsp. all-purpose flour
1¾ cups chicken stock
⅔ cup port or good-quality red wine
1 tbsp. freshly chopped thyme leaves, plus sprigs to garnish
1 bay leaf
4 tbsp. red currant jelly
salt and freshly ground black pepper
3 cups fresh penne
¾ cup grated Gruyère cheese

Tasty Tip

For a change, try specialty sausages for this recipe. Venison or wild boar sausages would work well with the rich sauce, as would Cumberland or spicy Cambridge pork sausages.

Pappardelle Pork with Brandy Sauce

1 Preheat the oven to 400° F. Using a sharp knife, cut two slits in each pork tenderloin, then stuff each slit with chopped sage. Season well with salt and pepper, and wrap each tenderloin with a slice of prosciutto.

2 Heat the olive oil in a large skillet. Add the wrapped pork fillets and cook, turning once, for 1–2 minutes or until the prosciutto is golden brown. Transfer to a roasting pan and cook in the preheated oven for 10–12 minutes.

3 Return the skillet to the heat and add the brandy, scraping the bottom of the pan with a spoon to release all the flavors. Boil for 1 minute, then pour in the chicken stock. Boil for an additional 2 minutes, then pour in the cream and boil again for 2–3 minutes or until the sauce has thickened slightly. Season the brandy sauce to taste.

4 Bring a large pan of lightly salted water to a rolling boil. Add the pasta and cook according to the package directions or until al dente. Drain the pasta thoroughly and return to the pan. Add the butter and chopped parsley, and toss together. Keep the pasta warm.

5 Remove the pork from the oven and pour any juices into the brandy sauce. Pile the pasta on individual plates and season with pepper. Spoon over the brandy sauce and serve immediately with the pork fillets.

INGREDIENTS
Serves 4

4 pork tenderloins, each weighing about 6 oz.

1 tbsp. freshly chopped sage, plus whole leaves to garnish

salt and freshly ground black pepper

4 slices prosciutto

1 tbsp. olive oil

6 tbsp. brandy

1¼ cups chicken stock

¾ cup heavy cream

12 oz. pappardelle

1–2 tsp. butter

2 tbsp. freshly chopped Italian parsley

Tasty Tip

An inexpensive French cooking brandy can be used for this recipe, but for a special occasion, use Calvados. Made from apples, it goes well with pork.

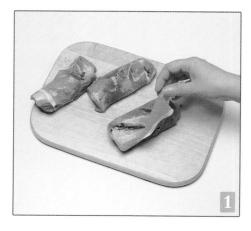

Tagliatelle with Spicy Sausage Ragù

1 Preheat the oven to 400° F. Heat 1 tablespoon of the olive oil in a large skillet. Prick the sausages, add to the pan, and cook for 8–10 minutes or until browned and cooked through. Remove and cut into thin diagonal slices. Set aside.

2 Return the pan to the heat and pour in the remaining olive oil. Add the onion and cook for 8 minutes or until softened. Add the fennel seeds and ground pork, and cook, stirring, for 5–8 minutes or until the meat is sealed and browned.

3 Stir in the tomatoes, tomato paste, and the wine or port. Season to taste with salt and pepper. Bring to a boil, cover, and simmer for 30 minutes, stirring occasionally. Remove the lid and simmer for 10 minutes.

4 Bring a large pan of lightly salted water to a rolling boil. Add the pasta and cook according to the package directions or until al dente. Drain thoroughly and toss with the meat sauce.

5 Place half the pasta in an ovenproof dish, and cover with 4 tablespoons of the white sauce. Top with half the sausages and grated Parmesan cheese. Repeat the layering, finishing with white sauce and Parmesan cheese. Bake in the preheated oven for 20 minutes, until golden brown. Serve immediately.

INGREDIENTS
Serves 4

3 tbsp. olive oil

6 spicy sausages

1 small onion, peeled and finely chopped

1 tsp. fennel seeds

2¼ cups fresh ground pork

8-oz. can chopped tomatoes with garlic

1 tbsp. sun-dried tomato paste

2 tbsp. red wine or port

salt and freshly ground black pepper

12 oz. tagliatelle

1¼ cups prepared white sauce (see page 98)

½ cup freshly grated Parmesan cheese

Helpful Hint

Most supermarkets sell cans of chopped tomatoes with added flavoring; if you cannot find them, simply add a large crushed garlic clove to regular canned tomatoes.

Food Fact

The sweet aniseed flavor of fennel seeds has an affinity with the slight acidity of tomatoes.

Pasta with Beef, Capers, & Olives

1 Heat the olive oil in a large skillet over a high heat. Add the steak and cook, stirring, for 3–4 minutes or until browned. Remove from the pan using a slotted spoon and set aside.

2 Lower the heat, add the scallions and garlic to the pan, and cook for 1 minute. Add the zucchini and bell pepper, and cook for 3–4 minutes.

3 Add the oregano, capers, and olives to the pan with the chopped tomatoes. Season to taste with salt and pepper, then simmer for 7 minutes, stirring occasionally. Return the beef to the pan and simmer for 3–5 minutes or until the sauce has thickened slightly.

4 Meanwhile, bring a large pan of lightly salted water to a rolling boil. Add the pasta and cook according to the package directions or until al dente.

5 Drain the pasta thoroughly. Return to the pan and add the beef sauce. Toss gently until the pasta is lightly coated. Spoon into a warmed serving dish or onto individual plates. Sprinkle with chopped parsley and serve immediately.

INGREDIENTS
Serves 4

2 tbsp. olive oil

11 oz. rump steak, trimmed and cut into strips

4 scallions, trimmed and sliced

2 garlic cloves, peeled and chopped

2 zucchini, trimmed and cut into strips

1 red bell pepper, deseeded and cut into strips

2 tsp. freshly chopped oregano

2 tbsp. capers, drained and rinsed

4 tbsp. pitted black olives, sliced

14-oz. can chopped tomatoes

salt and freshly ground black pepper

1 lb. fettuccine

1 tbsp. freshly chopped parsley, to garnish

Tasty Tip

When cooking the beef, it is important that it fries rather than steams in the pan, giving a beautifully brown and caramelized outside while keeping the middle moist and tender. Make sure that the oil in the pan is hot so that the strips of beef sizzle when added. Pat the beef dry with paper towels, and cook it in two batches so there is plenty of room to move it around the pan. Spoon the first batch onto a plate and set aside while cooking the second, then return to the pan with any juices.

Gnocchi & Prosciutto Bake

1 Heat the oven to 350° F. Heat 2 tablespoons of the olive oil in a large skillet and cook the onion and garlic for 5 minutes or until softened. Stir in the tomatoes, sun-dried tomato paste, and mascarpone cheese. Season to taste with salt and pepper. Add half the tarragon. Bring to a boil, then lower the heat immediately and simmer for 5 minutes.

2 Meanwhile, bring 8 cups water to a boil in a large pan. Add the remaining olive oil and a good pinch of salt. Add the gnocchi and cook for 1–2 minutes or until they rise to the surface.

3 Drain the gnocchi thoroughly and transfer to a large ovenproof dish. Add the tomato sauce and toss gently to coat the pasta. Combine the cheddar or Parmesan cheese with the bread crumbs and remaining tarragon and spread over the pasta mixture. Top with the prosciutto and olives and season again.

4 Cook in the preheated oven for 20–25 minutes, or until golden and bubbling. Serve immediately, garnished with parsley sprigs.

INGREDIENTS
Serves 4

3 tbsp. olive oil
1 red onion, peeled and sliced
2 garlic cloves, peeled
3 plum tomatoes, skinned and quartered
2 tbsp. sun-dried tomato paste
1 cup mascarpone cheese
salt and freshly ground black pepper
1 tbsp. freshly chopped tarragon
11 oz. fresh gnocchi
1 cup grated cheddar or Parmesan cheese
1 cup fresh white bread crumbs
2 oz. prosciutto, sliced
10 pitted green olives, halved
sprigs of Italian parsley, to garnish

Helpful Hint

Make sure that you buy gnocchi potato dumplings for this recipe and not gnocchi sardi, a pasta of a similar name. It is important to use a large pan of boiling water so that the gnocchi have plenty of room to move around, otherwise they will stick together during cooking. If you do not have a large enough pan, cook the gnocchi in two batches.

Chinese Beef with Angel Hair Pasta

1 Crush the peppercorns, using a mortar and pestle. Transfer to a shallow bowl and combine with the chili powder, Szechuan pepper, light soy sauce, and sherry. Add the beef strips and stir until lightly coated. Cover and place in the refrigerator to marinate for 3 hours; stir occasionally during this time.

2 When ready to cook, bring a large pan of lightly salted water to a boil. Add the pasta, and cook according to the package directions or until al dente. Drain and return to the pan. Add the sesame oil and toss lightly. Keep the pasta warm.

3 Heat a wok or large skillet, then add the sunflower oil and heat until very hot. Add the shredded scallions with the sliced red and green bell peppers, and stir-fry for 2 minutes.

4 Drain the beef, saving the marinade, then add the beef to the wok or skillet and stir-fry for 3 minutes. Pour the marinade, and stir-fry for 1-2 minutes or until the beef is tender.

5 Pile the pasta onto 4 warm plates. Top with the beef and bell peppers, then garnish with toasted sesame seeds and shredded scallions. Serve immediately.

INGREDIENTS
Serves 4

1 tbsp. pink peppercorns
1 tbsp. chili powder
1 tbsp. Szechuan pepper
3 tbsp. light soy sauce
3 tbsp. dry sherry
1 lb. sirloin steak, cut into strips
12 oz. angel-hair pasta
1 tbsp. sesame oil
1 tbsp. sunflower oil
1 bunch scallions, trimmed and finely shredded, plus extra to garnish
1 red bell pepper, deseeded and thinly sliced
1 green bell pepper, deseeded and thinly sliced
1 tbsp. toasted sesame seeds, to garnish

Food Fact

Szechuan pepper, which is also known as "Sichwan pepper," "anise pepper," and *fagara*, is not related in any way to black and white pepper. It is the reddish-brown, dried berry of the Chinese prickly ash tree and has a pronounced spicy, woody flavor. It is one of the essential ingredients of Chinese five-spice powder.

Lamb Arrabbiata

1 Heat 2 tablespoons of the olive oil in a large skillet and cook the lamb for 5–7 minutes or until sealed. Remove from the skillet using a slotted spoon and set aside.

2 Heat the remaining oil in the skillet. Add the onion, garlic, and chili, and cook until softened. Add the tomatoes and bring to a boil, then simmer for 10 minutes.

3 Return the browned lamb to the skillet with the olives and pour in the wine. Bring the sauce back to a boil, then reduce the heat and simmer, uncovered, for 15 minutes or until the lamb is tender. Season to taste with salt and pepper.

4 Meanwhile, bring a large pan of lightly salted water to a rolling boil. Add the pasta and cook according to the package directions or until al dente.

5 Drain the pasta. Toss in the butter, then add to the sauce and mix. Stir in 4 tablespoons of the chopped parsley, then spoon into a warmed serving dish. Sprinkle with the remaining parsley and serve immediately.

INGREDIENTS
Serves 4

4 tbsp. olive oil

1 lb. lamb fillets, cubed

1 large onion, peeled and sliced

4 garlic cloves, peeled and finely chopped

1 red chili, deseeded and finely chopped

14-oz. can chopped tomatoes

1½ cups black olives, pitted and halved

⅔ cup white wine

salt and freshly ground black pepper

2½ cups farfalle

1 tsp. butter

4 tbsp. freshly chopped parsley, plus 1 tbsp. to garnish

Food Fact

When cooking pasta, remember to use a very large pan so that the pasta has plenty of space to move around freely. Once the water has come to a boil, add the pasta and stir, then cover with a lid and return to a boil. The lid can then be removed so that the water does not boil over.

Helpful Hint

Lamb fillet can be quite fatty—cut off and discard as much fat as possible. If preferred, leg of lamb can be used instead.

Creamed Lamb & Wild Mushroom Pasta

1 Place the porcini in a small bowl and cover with almost-boiling water. Let soak for 30 minutes. Drain the porcini, saving the soaking liquid. Chop the porcini finely.

2 Bring a large pan of lightly salted water to a rolling boil. Add the pasta and cook according to the package directions or until al dente.

3 Meanwhile, melt the butter with the olive oil in a large skillet and fry the lamb to seal. Add the garlic, mushrooms, and prepared porcini, and cook for 5 minutes or until just soft.

4 Add the wine and the porcini soaking liquid, then simmer for 2 minutes. Stir in the cream with the seasoning and simmer for 1–2 minutes or until just thickened.

5 Drain the pasta thoroughly, setting aside about 4 tablespoons of the cooking water. Return the pasta to the pan. Pour over the mushroom sauce and toss lightly together, adding the pasta water if the sauce is too thick. Spoon into a warmed serving dish or onto individual plates. Garnish with the chopped parsley and serve immediately with grated Parmesan cheese.

INGREDIENTS
Serves 4
⅔ cup dried porcini

4 cups pasta shapes

2 tbsp. butter

1 tbsp. olive oil

12 oz. lamb neck fillet, thinly sliced

1 garlic clove, peeled and crushed

2½ cups brown or wild mushrooms, wiped and sliced

4 tbsp. white wine

½ cup heavy cream

salt and freshly ground black pepper

1 tbsp. freshly chopped parsley, to garnish

freshly grated Parmesan cheese, to serve

Helpful Hint

Dried porcini mushrooms have a rich, intense flavor. After soaking, they should be briefly rinsed to remove any grit or dirt. Strain the soaking liquid through a cheesecloth or a very fine sieve. If you do not have either of these, leave it to settle for about 10 minutes; grit will sink to the bottom and the liquid can be poured off, leaving any sediment behind.

Tagliatelle with Creamy Liver & Basil

1 Season the flour lightly with salt and pepper and place in a large plastic bag. Add the liver and toss gently to coat. Remove the liver from the bag and set aside.

2 Melt the butter with the olive oil in a large skillet. Add the onion and garlic, and fry for 6–8 minutes or until the onions begin to brown. Add the liver and fry until brown on all sides.

3 Stir in the chicken stock, tomato paste, and sun-dried tomatoes. Bring to a boil, then reduce the heat and simmer very gently for 10 minutes.

4 Meanwhile, bring a large pan of lightly salted water to a rolling boil. Add the pasta and cook according to the package directions or until al dente.

5 Stir the chopped basil and cream into the liver sauce and season to taste.

6 Drain the pasta thoroughly, setting aside 2 tablespoons of the cooking water. Spoon the pasta into a warmed serving dish or pile onto individual plates. Stir the reserved cooking water into the liver sauce and pour over the pasta. Toss lightly to coat the pasta. Garnish with basil leaves and serve immediately.

INGREDIENTS
Serves 4

2 tbsp. all-purpose flour
salt and freshly ground black pepper
1 lb. lamb's liver, thinly sliced and cut into bite-sized pieces (use calf's liver if lamb's liver is unavailable)
2 tbsp. butter
1 tbsp. olive oil
2 red onions, peeled and sliced
1 garlic clove, peeled and sliced
⅔ cup chicken stock
1 tbsp. tomato paste
2 sun-dried tomatoes, finely chopped
1 tbsp. freshly chopped basil
⅔ cup heavy cream
12 oz. tagliatelle verde
fresh basil leaves, to garnish

Helpful Hint

Although not as delicately flavored as calf's liver, lamb's liver can be wonderfully tender and moist if gently simmered, as shown here. To tone down the flavor, it can be soaked in a little milk for 1 hour after preparation. Drain the liver and pat it dry on paper towels before cooking.

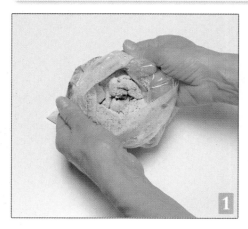

Ham Steak with Red Wine Sauce & Pasta

1 Preheat the broiler to a medium heat before cooking. Heat the butter with the red wine in a large heavy-based pan. Add the onions and cover with a tight-fitting lid. Cook over a very low heat for 30 minutes or until softened and transparent. Remove the lid from the pan then stir in the orange juice and sugar. Increase the heat, and cook for about 10 minutes or until the onions are golden.

2 Meanwhile, cook the ham steak under the preheated broiler, turning at least once, for 4–6 minutes or until tender. Cut the cooked ham into bite-sized pieces. Set aside and keep warm.

3 Meanwhile, bring a large pan of very lightly salted water to a rolling boil. Add the pasta and cook according to the package directions or until al dente. Drain the pasta, then return it to the pan. Season with a little black pepper and keep warm.

4 Stir the whole-grain mustard and chopped parsley into the onion sauce, then pour over the pasta. Add the ham pieces to the pan and toss lightly to thoroughly coat the pasta with the sauce. Pile the pasta mixture onto two warmed serving plates. Garnish with sprigs of Italian parsley and serve immediately.

INGREDIENTS
Serves 2

2 tbsp. butter
⅔ cup red wine
4 red onions, peeled and sliced
4 tbsp. orange juice
1 tsp. soft brown sugar
8 oz. ham steak, trimmed
1½ cups fusilli
freshly ground black pepper
3 tbsp. whole-grain mustard
2 tbsp. freshly chopped Italian parsley, plus sprigs to garnish

Helpful Hint

Ham steak can be slightly salty, so add only a little salt when cooking the pasta. Whole-grain mustard is made from mixed mustard seeds. This gives it a grainy texture and a fruity, spicy flavor that goes particularly well with ham steak.

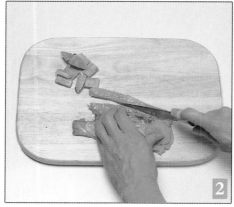

Prosciutto & Gruyère Carbonara

1 Place the egg yolks with 6 tablespoons of the Gruyère cheese in a bowl and mix lightly until well blended, then set aside.

2 Heat the olive oil in a large pan, and cook the garlic and shallots for 5 minutes or until golden-brown. Add the prosciutto ham, then cook for an additional minute. Pour in the dry vermouth and simmer for 2 minutes, then remove from the heat. Season to taste with salt and pepper and keep warm.

3 Meanwhile, bring a large pan of lightly salted water to a rolling boil. Add the pasta and cook according to the package directions or until al dente. Drain thoroughly, setting aside 4 tablespoons of the water, and return the pasta to the pan.

4 Remove from the heat, then add the egg and cheese mixture with the butter to the pasta; toss lightly until coated. Add the prosciutto mixture and toss again, adding the pasta water, if needed, to moisten. Season to taste and sprinkle with the remaining Gruyère cheese and the shredded basil leaves. Garnish with basil sprigs and serve immediately.

INGREDIENTS
Serves 4

3 medium egg yolks
½ cup grated Gruyère cheese
2 tbsp. olive oil
2 garlic cloves, peeled and crushed
2 shallots, peeled and finely chopped
7 oz. prosciutto ham, cut into strips
4 tbsp. dry vermouth
salt and freshly ground black pepper
1 lb. spaghetti
1 tbsp. butter
1 tbsp. freshly shredded basil leaves
basil sprigs, to garnish

Food Fact

Gruyère cheese is now produced in many countries, including the United States and France. It is named after the Swiss mountain village where it originated and is still made. The pale yellow cheese is pitted with pea-sized holes and has a firm texture and a sweet, slightly nutty taste.

Gnocchi with Tuscan Beef Ragù

1 Preheat the oven to 400° F. Place the porcini in a small bowl and cover with almost-boiling water. Let soak for 30 minutes. Drain, setting aside the soaking liquid and straining it through a cheesecloth-lined sieve. Chop the porcini.

2 Heat the olive oil in a large heavy-based pan. Add the onion, carrot, celery, fennel, and garlic, and cook, stirring, for 8 minutes or until soft. Add the ground beef and cook, stirring, for 5–8 minutes or until sealed and any lumps are broken up.

3 Pour in the wine, then add the porcini with half the pine nuts, the rosemary, and tomato paste. Stir in the porcini soaking liquid, then simmer for 5 minutes. Add the chopped tomatoes and simmer gently for about 40 minutes, stirring occasionally.

4 Meanwhile, bring 8 cups of lightly salted water to a rolling boil in a large pan. Add the gnocchi and cook for 1–2 minutes, until they rise to the surface.

5 Drain the gnocchi and place in an ovenproof dish. Stir in three-quarters of the mozzarella cheese with the beef sauce. Season to taste. Top with the remaining mozzarella and pine nuts, then bake in the preheated oven for 20 minutes until golden brown. Serve immediately.

INGREDIENTS
Serves 4

⅔ cup dried porcini

3 tbsp. olive oil

1 small onion, peeled and finely chopped

1 carrot, peeled and finely chopped

1 celery, trimmed and finely chopped

1 fennel bulb, trimmed and sliced

2 garlic cloves, peeled and crushed

1 lb. fresh ground beef

4 tbsp. red wine

⅓ cup pine nuts

1 tbsp. freshly chopped rosemary

2 tbsp. tomato paste

14-oz. can chopped tomatoes

1 cup cubed mozzarella cheese

salt and freshly ground black pepper

8 oz. fresh gnocchi

Food Fact

Pine nuts are small, creamy-colored, tear-shaped nuts from the base of the cone scales of the Mediterranean stone pine. Due to their high oil content, they may become rancid if kept too long, so buy in small amounts and use within 1–2 months.

Hot Duck Pasta Salad

1 Preheat the oven to 400° F. Place the duck breasts on a cookie sheet lined with foil. Mix together the mustard and honey, and season lightly with salt and pepper, then spread over the duck breasts. Roast in the preheated oven for 20–30 minutes or until tender. Remove from the oven and keep warm.

2 Meanwhile, place the eggs in a small pan, then cover with water and bring to a boil. Simmer for 8 minutes, then drain. Bring a large pan of lightly salted water to a rolling boil. Add the beans and pasta, then return to a boil and cook according to the package directions or until al dente. Drain the pasta and beans and refresh under cold running water.

3 Place the pasta and beans in a bowl. Add the carrot, corn, and spinach leaves, and toss lightly. Shell the eggs, then cut into wedges and arrange on top of the pasta. Slice the duck breasts, then place them on top of the salad. Beat the dressing ingredients together in a bowl until well blended, then drizzle over the salad. Serve immediately.

INGREDIENTS
Serves 6

3 boneless and skinless duck breasts
1 tbsp. whole-grain mustard
1 tbsp. clear honey
salt and freshly ground black pepper
4 medium eggs
4 cups fusilli
⅔ cup trimmed green beans
1 large carrot, peeled and thinly sliced
1 cup corn kernels, cooked if frozen
1 cup shredded fresh baby spinach leaves

FOR THE DRESSING:

8 tbsp. French dressing
1 tsp. horseradish sauce
4 tbsp. crème fraîche

Helpful Hint

Eggs should never be boiled rapidly, since this may cause the shells to crack and make the egg white rubbery. When cooking hard-boiled eggs for salads, turn the eggs gently once or twice in the first few minutes of cooking, so that the yolks stay in the middle. As soon as the eggs are cooked, remove them from the pan and place in a bowl of very cold water to prevent dark rings from forming around the yolk.

Chicken Tagliatelle

1 Bring a large pan of lightly salted water to a rolling boil. Add the pasta and cook according to the package directions or until al dente. Add the peas to the pan 5 minutes before the end of cooking time and cook until tender. Drain the pasta and peas, then return to the pan and keep warm.

2 Trim the chicken if necessary, then cut into bite-sized pieces. Heat the olive oil in a large skillet, then add the chicken and cook for 8 minutes or until golden, stirring occasionally.

3 Add the cucumber and cook for 2 minutes or until slightly softened, stirring occasionally. Stir in the vermouth and bring to a boil, then lower the heat and simmer for 3 minutes or until reduced slightly.

4 Add the cream to the pan. Bring to a boil, stirring constantly, then stir in the Stilton cheese and cut chives. Season to taste with salt and pepper. Heat through well, stirring occasionally, until the cheese begins to melt.

5 Toss the chicken mixture into the pasta. Spoon into a warmed serving dish or onto individual plates. Garnish and serve immediately.

INGREDIENTS
Serves 4

12 oz. tagliatelle
1 cup frozen peas
4 boneless and skinless chicken breasts
2 tbsp. olive oil
¼ cucumber, cut into strips
⅔ cup dry vermouth
⅔ cup heavy cream
1 cup crumbled Stilton cheese
3 tbsp. freshly cut chives, plus extra to garnish
salt and freshly ground black pepper
fresh herbs, to garnish

Helpful Hint

Chives add a mild onion flavor and attractive color to this dish. If you do not have any, finely shred the green tops of scallions and use them instead. If preferred, a mixture of dry white wine and 1–2 tablespoons of dry sherry can be substituted for the vermouth.

Mixed Vegetable & Chicken Pasta

1 Preheat the broiler just before using. Cut the chicken into thin strips. Trim the leeks, leaving some of the dark green tops, then shred and wash in cold water. Peel the onion and cut into thin wedges.

2 Bring a large pan of lightly salted water to a rolling boil. Add the pasta and cook according to the package directions or until al dente.

3 Meanwhile, melt the butter with the olive oil in a large heavy-based pan. Add the chicken and cook, stirring occasionally, for 8 minutes or until browned all over. Add the leeks and onion, and cook for 5 minutes or until softened. Add the garlic and cherry tomatoes, and cook for an additional 2 minutes.

4 Stir the cream and asparagus tips into the chicken and vegetable mixture, and bring to a boil slowly, then remove from the heat. Drain the pasta and return to the pan. Pour the sauce over the pasta, and season to taste with salt and pepper, then toss lightly.

5 Spoon the mixture into a gratin dish and sprinkle with the cheese. Cook under the preheated broiler for 5 minutes or until bubbling and golden, turning the dish occasionally. Serve with a green salad.

INGREDIENTS
Serves 4

3 boneless and skinless chicken breasts
2 leeks
1 red onion
3 cups pasta shells
2 tbsp. butter
2 tbsp. olive oil
1 garlic clove, peeled and chopped
6 oz. cherry tomatoes, halved
¾ cup heavy cream
15-oz. can asparagus tips, drained
salt and freshly ground black pepper
1 cup crumbled Double Gloucester cheese with chives
green salad, to serve

Tasty Tip

Fresh asparagus is in season during May and June, and can be used in place of canned asparagus. Tie in small bundles and cook in lightly salted, boiling water for 5–8 minutes.

Herb-Baked Chicken with Tagliatelle

1 Preheat the oven to 400° F. Mix together the bread crumbs, 1 tablespoon of the olive oil, the oregano, and tomato paste. Season to taste with salt and pepper. Place the chicken breasts well apart in a roasting pan, and coat with the bread-crumb mixture.

2 Mix the plum tomatoes with the chopped basil and white wine. Season to taste, then spoon evenly around the chicken.

3 Drizzle the remaining olive oil over the chicken breasts and cook in the preheated oven for 20–30 minutes or until the chicken is golden and the juices run clear when a skewer is inserted into the flesh.

4 Meanwhile, bring a large pan of lightly salted water to a rolling boil. Add the pasta and cook according to the package directions or until al dente.

5 Drain the pasta thoroughly and transfer to warmed serving plates. Arrange the chicken breasts on top of the pasta and spoon over the sauce. Garnish with sprigs of basil and serve immediately.

INGREDIENTS
Serves 4

1½ cups fresh white bread crumbs
3 tbsp. olive oil
1 tsp. dried oregano
2 tbsp. sun-dried tomato paste
salt and freshly ground black
  pepper
4 boneless and skinless chicken
  breasts, each about 5 oz.
2 14-oz. cans plum tomatoes
4 tbsp. freshly chopped basil
2 tbsp. dry white wine
12 oz. tagliatelle
fresh basil sprigs, to garnish

Food Fact

Sun-dried tomatoes are ripened on the vine, then split open and dried in the sun to give a deep, concentrated caramelized flavor. Sun-dried tomato paste usually comes in glass jars, but can also be found in tubes. Once opened, store in the refrigerator, and if in a jar, cover the surface with a teaspoon of olive oil to keep fresh.

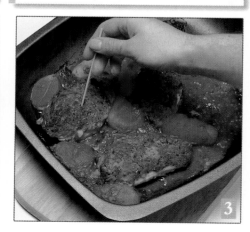

Creamy Chicken &
Sausage Penne

1 Heat the olive oil in a large skillet, then add the shallots and cook for 3 minutes or until golden. Remove and drain on paper towels. Add the chicken thighs to the skillet and cook for 5 minutes, turning frequently until browned. Drain on paper towels.

2 Add the smoked sausage and chestnut mushrooms to the skillet and cook for 3 minutes or until browned. Drain separately on paper towels.

3 Return the shallots, chicken, and sausage to the skillet, then add the garlic, paprika, and thyme, and cook for 1 minute, stirring. Pour in the wine and stock and season to taste with the pepper. Bring to a boil, then lower the heat and simmer covered for 15 minutes.

4 Add the mushrooms to the skillet and simmer covered for 15 minutes or until the chicken is tender.

5 Meanwhile, bring a large pan of lightly salted water to a rolling boil. Add the penne and cook according to the package directions or until al dente. Drain thoroughly.

6 Stir the mascarpone cheese into the chicken sauce and heat through, stirring gently. Spoon the pasta onto a warmed serving dish, and add the sauce. Garnish and serve immediately.

INGREDIENTS
Serves 4

2 tbsp. olive oil
8 oz. shallots, peeled
8 chicken thighs
6 oz. smoked sausage, thickly sliced
1¼ cups chestnut mushrooms, wiped and halved
2 garlic cloves, peeled and chopped
1 tbsp. paprika
1 small bunch fresh thyme, chopped, plus leaves to garnish
⅔ cup red wine
1¼ cups chicken stock
freshly ground black pepper
3 cups penne
1 cup mascarpone cheese

Food Fact

Mascarpone is a rich, soft, white cheese, more like cream than cheese. Its slightly sweet flavor means that it is frequently used in desserts, but it also makes a wonderfully smooth, quick sauce for cooked pasta since it simply melts in the heat.

Creamy Turkey & Tomato Pasta

1 Preheat the oven to 400° F. Heat 2 tablespoons of the olive oil in a large skillet. Add the turkey and cook for 5 minutes or until sealed, turning occasionally. Transfer to a roasting pan and add the remaining olive oil, the vine tomatoes, garlic, and balsamic vinegar. Stir well and season to taste with salt and pepper. Cook in the preheated oven for 30 minutes or until the turkey is tender, turning the tomatoes and turkey once.

2 Meanwhile, bring a large pan of lightly salted water to a rolling boil. Add the pasta and cook according to the package directions or until al dente. Drain, return to the pan, and keep warm. Stir the basil and seasoning into the crème fraîche.

3 Remove the roasting pan from the oven and discard the vines. Stir the crème fraîche and basil mix into the turkey and tomato mixture and return to the oven for 1–2 minutes or until thoroughly heated through.

4 Stir the turkey and tomato mixture into the pasta and toss lightly together. Spoon into a warmed serving dish. Garnish with Parmesan cheese shavings and serve immediately.

INGREDIENTS
Serves 4

4 tbsp. olive oil

1 lb. turkey breasts, cut into bite-sized pieces

1¼ lb. cherry tomatoes, on the vine

2 garlic cloves, peeled and chopped

4 tbsp. balsamic vinegar

12 oz. tagliatelle

salt and freshly ground black pepper

4 tbsp. freshly chopped basil

¾ cup crème fraîche

shaved Parmesan cheese, to garnish

Helpful Hint

Balsamic vinegar is dark in color with a mellow, sweet-and-sour flavor. It is made from concentrated grape juice and fermented in wooden barrels. Like good wine, the vinegar improves and becomes darker and more syrupy the longer it is aged. Less expensive vinegars bought from supermarkets have been matured for only three or four years. The flavor is nonetheless wonderful and perfect for this recipe.

Prosciutto-Wrapped Chicken with Ribbon Pasta

1 Cut each chicken breast into three pieces and season well with salt and pepper. Wrap each chicken piece in a slice of prosciutto to enclose completely, securing if necessary with either fine twine or toothpicks.

2 Heat the oil in a large skillet and cook the chicken, turning occasionally, for 12–15 minutes or until well cooked. Remove from the skillet with a slotted spoon and set aside.

3 Meanwhile, bring a large pan of lightly salted water to a rolling boil. Add the pasta and cook according to the package directions or until al dente.

4 Add the garlic and scallions to the skillet and cook, stirring occasionally, for 2 minutes or until softened. Stir in the tomatoes, lemon juice, and crème fraîche. Bring to a boil, then lower the heat and simmer, covered, for 3 minutes. Stir in the parsley and sugar, then season to taste. Return the chicken to the skillet and heat for 2–3 minutes or until piping hot.

5 Drain the pasta thoroughly and mix in the chopped parsley, then spoon onto a warmed serving dish or individual plates. Arrange the chicken and sauce over the pasta. Garnish and serve immediately.

INGREDIENTS
Serves 4

4 boneless and skinless chicken
  breasts
salt and freshly ground black
  pepper
12 slices prosciutto
2 tbsp. olive oil
12 oz. ribbon pasta
1 garlic clove, peeled and chopped
1 bunch scallions, trimmed and
  diagonally sliced
14-oz. can chopped tomatoes
juice of 1 lemon
⅔ cup crème fraîche
3 tbsp. freshly chopped parsley
pinch of sugar
freshly grated Parmesan cheese, to
  garnish

Food Fact

Crème fraîche has a slightly sour taste and a thick, spoonable texture. It is made in a similar way to yogurt, by introducing a bacterial culture to cream. This produces lactic acid, which makes the cream curdle and thicken. The half-fat version is best avoided for cooking; it sometimes separates when boiled.

Baked Eggplant with Tomato & Mozzarella

1 Preheat the oven to 400° F. Place the eggplant slices in a colander and sprinkle with salt. Let stand for 1 hour or until the juices run clear. Rinse and dry on paper towels.

2 Heat 3–5 tablespoons of the oil in a large skillet, and cook the prepared eggplants in batches for 2 minutes on each side or until softened. Remove and drain on paper towels.

3 Heat 1 tablespoon of olive oil in a pan, then add the ground turkey and cook for 5 minutes or until browned and sealed.

4 Add the onion to the pan and cook for 5 minutes or until softened. Add the chopped garlic, tomatoes, and mixed herbs. Pour in the wine and season to taste with salt and pepper. Bring to a boil, then lower the heat and simmer for 15 minutes or until thickened.

5 Meanwhile, bring a large pan of lightly salted water to a rolling boil. Add the macaroni, and cook according to the package directions or until al dente. Drain thoroughly.

6 Spoon half the tomato mixture into a lightly greased ovenproof dish. Top with half the eggplant, pasta, and chopped basil, then season lightly. Repeat the layers, finishing with a layer of eggplant. Sprinkle with the mozzarella and Parmesan cheeses, then bake in the preheated oven for 30 minutes or until golden and bubbling. Serve immediately.

INGREDIENTS
Serves 4

3 medium eggplants, trimmed and sliced
salt and freshly ground black pepper
4–6 tbsp. olive oil
1 lb. fresh ground turkey
1 onion, peeled and chopped
2 garlic cloves, peeled and chopped
2 14-oz. cans cherry tomatoes
1 tbsp. fresh mixed herbs
¾ cup red wine
3 cups macaroni
5 tbsp. freshly chopped basil
1 cup mozzarella cheese
½ cup freshly grated Parmesan cheese

Helpful Hint

Eggplants are salted to remove bitterness, although they are now less bitter. Salting also removes moisture so they absorb less oil when fried.

Mini Chicken Balls with Tagliatelle

1 Mix the chicken and tomatoes together and season with salt and pepper. Divide the mixture into 32 pieces and roll into balls. Transfer to a cookie sheet, then cover and refrigerate for 1 hour.

2 Melt the butter in a large skillet. Add the chicken balls and cook for 5 minutes or until golden, turning occasionally. Remove, drain on paper towels, and keep warm.

3 Add the leeks and fava beans to the skillet and cook, stirring, for 10 minutes or until tender. Return the chicken balls to the skillet, then stir in the cream and Parmesan cheese and heat through.

4 Meanwhile, bring a large pan of lightly salted water to a boil. Add the pasta and cook according to the package directions or until al dente.

5 Bring a separate skilletful of water to a boil, then crack in the eggs and simmer for 2–4 minutes or until poached to personal preference.

6 Meanwhile, drain the pasta and return to the pan. Pour the chicken ball and vegetable sauce over the pasta, then toss lightly and heat for 1–2 minutes. Arrange on warmed individual plates and top with the poached eggs. Garnish with fresh herbs and serve immediately.

INGREDIENTS
Serves 4

1 lb. fresh ground chicken
½ cup sun-dried tomatoes, drained and finely chopped
salt and freshly ground black pepper
2 tbsp. butter
12 oz. leeks, trimmed and diagonally sliced
1 cup frozen fava beans
1¼ cups light cream
½ cup freshly grated Parmesan cheese
12 oz. tagliatelle
4 medium eggs
fresh herbs, to garnish

Helpful Hint

Chilling the chicken balls firms them, so that they retain their shape when cooked. They need plenty of room for turning; if necessary, cook in two batches, halving the butter for each. The butter must be sizzling before the chicken balls are added.

Pasta & Bell Pepper Salad

1 Preheat the oven to 400° F. Spoon the olive oil into a roasting pan and heat in the oven for 2 minutes or until almost smoking. Remove from the oven, then add the bell peppers, zucchini, and eggplant, and stir until coated. Bake for 30 minutes or until charred, stirring occasionally.

2 Bring a large pan of lightly salted water to a boil. Add the pasta and cook according to the package directions or until al dente. Drain and refresh under cold running water. Drain thoroughly, then place in a large salad bowl and set aside.

3 Remove the cooked vegetables from the oven and let cool. Add to the cooled pasta, together with the quartered tomatoes, chopped basil leaves, pesto, garlic, and lemon juice. Toss lightly to mix.

4 Shred the chicken coarsely into small pieces and stir into the pasta and vegetable mixture. Season to taste with salt and pepper, then sprinkle the crumbled feta cheese over the pasta and stir gently. Cover the dish and let marinate for 30 minutes, stirring occasionally. Serve the salad with fresh, crusty bread.

INGREDIENTS
Serves 4

4 tbsp. olive oil

1 each red, orange, and yellow bell pepper, deseeded and cut into chunks

1 large zucchini, trimmed and cut into chunks

1 medium eggplant, trimmed and diced

2½ cups fusilli

4 plum tomatoes, quartered

1 bunch fresh basil leaves, coarsely chopped

2 tbsp. pesto

2 garlic cloves, peeled and coarsely chopped

1 tbsp. lemon juice

8 oz. boneless and skinless roasted chicken breast

salt and freshly ground black pepper

1 cup crumbled feta cheese

fresh, crusty bread, to serve

Helpful Hint

If you have one, use a large nonstick roasting pan for cooking the vegetables, and check and move them around frequently so that they brown evenly. For extra flavor, use a garlic- or chili-flavored olive oil and tuck a sprig or two of fresh herbs, such as rosemary or thyme, under the vegetables.

Chicken Marengo

1 Season the flour with salt and pepper and toss the chicken in the flour to coat. Heat 2 tablespoons of the olive oil in a large skillet and cook the chicken for 7 minutes or until browned, turning occasionally. Remove from the skillet using a slotted spoon and keep warm.

2 Add the remaining oil to the skillet, then add the onion and cook, stirring occasionally, for 5 minutes or until softened and starting to brown. Add the garlic, tomatoes, tomato paste, basil, and thyme. Pour in the wine or chicken stock and season well. Bring to a boil. Stir in the

chicken pieces, and simmer for 15 minutes or until the chicken is tender and the sauce has thickened.

3 Meanwhile, bring a large pan of lightly salted water to a boil. Add the rigatoni and cook according to the package directions or until al dente.

4 Drain the rigatoni thoroughly, then return to the pan and stir in the chopped parsley. Tip the pasta into a large, warmed serving dish or spoon onto individual plates. Spoon the chicken sauce over the pasta and serve immediately.

INGREDIENTS
Serves 4

2 tbsp. all-purpose flour
salt and freshly ground black pepper
4 boneless and skinless chicken breasts, cut into bite-sized pieces
4 tbsp. olive oil
1 Spanish onion, peeled and chopped
1 garlic clove, peeled and chopped
14-oz. can chopped tomatoes
2 tbsp. sun-dried tomato paste
3 tbsp. freshly chopped basil
3 tbsp. freshly chopped thyme
½ cup dry white wine or chicken stock
3 cups rigatoni
3 tbsp. freshly chopped Italian parsley

Helpful Hint

Spanish onions have a milder flavor and tend to be larger than others. Cook the onion over a fairly low heat until really soft, stirring frequently toward the end to keep it from sticking. Let it caramelize and brown very slightly, as this adds a richer flavor and golden color to the final dish.

Turkey & Oven-Roasted Vegetable Salad

1 Preheat the oven to 400° F. Line a large roasting pan with foil, then pour in half the olive oil and place in the oven for 3 minutes or until very hot. Remove from the oven, add the zucchini and bell peppers, and stir until evenly coated. Bake for 30–35 minutes or until slightly charred, turning occasionally.

2 Add the pine nuts to the pan. Return to the oven and bake for 10 minutes or until the pine nuts are toasted. Remove from the oven and let the vegetables cool completely.

3 Bring a large pan of lightly salted water to a rolling boil. Add the macaroni and cook according to the package directions or until al dente. Drain and rinse the pasta under cold running water, then drain thoroughly and place in a large salad bowl.

4 Cut the turkey into bite-size pieces and add to the macaroni. Add the artichokes and tomatoes with the cooled vegetables and pan juices to the pan. Blend together the cilantro, garlic, remaining oil, vinegar, and seasoning. Pour over the salad, then toss lightly and serve.

INGREDIENTS
Serves 4

6 tbsp. olive oil

3 medium zucchini, trimmed and sliced

2 yellow bell peppers, deseeded and sliced

½ cup pine nuts

2½ cups macaroni

12 oz. cooked turkey

10 oz. jar or can of chargrilled artichokes, drained and sliced

8 oz. baby plum tomatoes, quartered

4 tbsp. freshly chopped cilantro

1 garlic clove, peeled and chopped

3 tbsp. balsamic vinegar

salt and freshly ground black pepper

Helpful Hint

Other vegetables would be equally delicious. Try baby eggplants, trimmed and quartered lengthwise, or scrubbed new potatoes. If you cannot find chargrilled artichokes, use ordinary ones: drain and pat dry, then add to 1 tablespoon of hot olive oil in a skillet and cook for 2–3 minutes or until lightly charred.

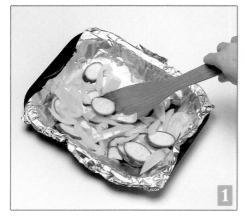

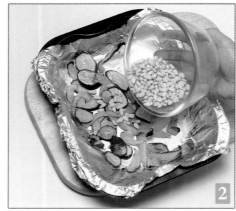

Spicy Chicken & Pasta Salad

1 Bring a large pan of lightly salted water to a rolling boil. Add the pasta shells and cook according to the package directions or until al dente. Drain and refresh under cold running water, then drain thoroughly and place in a large serving bowl.

2 Meanwhile, melt the butter in a heavy-based pan, then add the onion and cook for 5 minutes or until softened. Add the curry paste and cook, stirring, for 2 minutes. Stir in the apricots and tomato paste, then cook for 1 minute. Remove from the heat and let cool.

3 Blend the mango chutney and mayonnaise together in a small bowl. Drain the pineapple slices, adding 2 tablespoons of the pineapple juice to the mayonnaise mixture; set aside the pineapple slices. Season the mayonnaise to taste with salt and pepper.

4 Cut the pineapple slices into chunks and stir into the pasta together with the mayonnaise mixture, curry paste, and cooked chicken pieces. Toss lightly together to coat the pasta. Sprinkle with the almond slivers, then garnish with cilantro sprigs and serve.

INGREDIENTS
Serves 6

4 cups pasta shells
4 tbsp. butter
1 onion, peeled and chopped
2 tbsp. mild curry paste
1 cup chopped dried apricots
2 tbsp. tomato paste
3 tbsp. mango chutney
1¼ cups mayonnaise
15-oz. can pineapple slices in juice
salt and freshly ground black pepper
1 lb. skinned, boned, cooked chicken, cut into bite-size pieces
2 tbsp. almond slivers, flaked and toasted
cilantro sprigs, to garnish

Helpful Hint

If you cannot buy slivered almonds, prepare your own. Place whole or half-blanched almonds in a small bowl and pour in plenty of boiling water. Let soak for 20 minutes, then drain the almonds and cut into slivers using a sharp knife. Spread on a foil-lined broiler pan and toast under a low broiler for 1–2 minutes to make them dry and crunchy again.

Chicken, Gorgonzola, & Mushroom Macaroni

1 Bring a large pan of lightly salted water to a rolling boil. Add the macaroni and cook according to the package directions or until al dente.

2 Meanwhile, melt the butter in a large skillet, then add the chestnut and button mushrooms and cook for 5 minutes or until golden, stirring occasionally. Add the chicken to the skillet and cook for 4 minutes or until heated through and slightly golden, stirring occasionally.

3 Blend the cornstarch with a little of the milk in a pitcher to form a smooth paste, then gradually blend in the remaining milk and pour into the skillet. Bring to a boil slowly, stirring constantly. Add the Gorgonzola cheese and cook for 1 minute, stirring frequently until melted.

4 Stir the sage and chives into the skillet. Season to taste with salt and pepper, then heat through. Drain the macaroni and return to the pan. Pour the chicken and mushroom sauce over the macaroni and toss lightly to coat. Spoon into a warmed serving dish, and serve immediately with extra Gorgonzola cheese.

INGREDIENTS
Serves 4

4 cups macaroni
¾ stick butter
2½ cups chestnut mushrooms, wiped and sliced
2½ cups baby button mushrooms, wiped and halved
12 oz. cooked chicken, skinned and chopped
2 tsp. cornstarch
1¼ cups low-fat milk
1/2 cup chopped Gorgonzola cheese, plus extra to serve
2 tbsp. freshly chopped sage
1 tbsp. freshly chopped chives, plus extra chive leaves to garnish
salt and freshly ground black pepper

Food Fact

First mentioned in A.D. 879, Gorgonzola is the oldest named cheese in the world. It was named after the Italian town where cattle rested on their annual return from their summer pastures to their winter stalls. The original *piccante* is firm and heavily blue-veined with a strong flavor, while *dolce*, often simply labeled "extra creamy," has a milder taste and a softer texture.

Spaghetti with Turkey & Bacon Sauce

1 Bring a large pan of lightly salted water to a rolling boil. Add the spaghetti and cook according to the package directions or until al dente.

2 Meanwhile, melt the butter in a large skillet. Using a sharp knife, dice the bacon into small pieces. Add the bacon to the skillet with the turkey strips and cook for 8 minutes or until browned, stirring occasionally to prevent sticking. Add the onion and garlic, and cook for 5 minutes or until softened, stirring occasionally.

3 Place the eggs and cream in a bowl and season to taste with salt and pepper. Beat together, then pour into the skillet and cook, stirring, for 2 minutes or until the mixture begins to thicken but does not scramble.

4 Drain the spaghetti thoroughly and return to the pan. Pour over the sauce, then add the Parmesan cheese and toss lightly. Heat through for 2 minutes or until piping hot. Spoon into a warmed serving dish and sprinkle with freshly chopped cilantro. Serve immediately.

INGREDIENTS
Serves 4

1 lb. spaghetti
2 tbsp. butter
8 oz. smoked bacon
12 oz. fresh turkey strips
1 onion, peeled and chopped
1 garlic clove, peeled and chopped
3 medium eggs, beaten
1¼ cups heavy cream
salt and freshly ground black
  pepper
½ cup freshly grated Parmesan
  cheese
2–3 tbsp. freshly chopped cilantro,
  to garnish

Helpful Hint

It is a good idea to remove the skillet from the heat before adding the beaten eggs, since there should be enough residual heat in the sauce to cook them. If the sauce does not start to thicken after 2 minutes, return to a very low heat and continue cooking gently until it does.

Cheesy Baked Chicken Macaroni

1 Preheat the broiler just before cooking. Heat the oil in a large skillet, and cook the chicken for 8 minutes or until browned, stirring occasionally. Drain on paper towels and set aside. Add the diced pancetta to the skillet, and fry until browned and crispy. Remove from the skillet and set aside.

2 Add the onion and garlic to the skillet, and cook for 5 minutes or until softened. Stir in the tomato sauce, chopped tomatoes, and basil, and season to taste with salt and pepper. Bring to a boil, lower the heat, and simmer the sauce for about 5 minutes.

3 Meanwhile, bring a large pan of lightly salted water to a boil. Add the macaroni and cook according to the package directions or until al dente.

4 Drain the macaroni thoroughly, then return to the pan and stir in the sauce, chicken, and mozzarella. Spoon into a shallow ovenproof dish.

5 Sprinkle the pancetta over the macaroni. Sprinkle the Gruyère and Parmesan cheeses on top. Place under the preheated broiler and cook for 5–10 minutes or until golden-brown; turn the dish occasionally. Garnish and serve immediately.

INGREDIENTS
Serves 4

1 tbsp. olive oil
3¾ cups diced boneless and skinless chicken breasts
⅓ cup diced pancetta
1 onion, peeled and chopped
1 garlic clove, peeled and chopped
1½ cups tomato sauce
14-oz. can chopped tomatoes
2 tbsp. freshly chopped basil, plus leaves to garnish
salt and freshly ground black pepper
3 cups macaroni
1¼ cups drained and chopped mozzarella cheese
½ cup grated Gruyère cheese
½ cup freshly grated Parmesan cheese

Tasty Tip

This dish can be made with any pasta shape or flavor; try green spinach pasta for a change. Check the contents of the package of fresh tomato sauce carefully; it may already contain herbs and spices, so you may need to cut out or reduce the garlic and fresh basil accordingly.

Food Fact

Pancetta (unsmoked bacon) imparts a wonderful flavor to a dish; it is available from Italian delicatessens.

Spicy Mexican Chicken

1 Heat the oil in a large skillet, then add the ground chicken and cook for 5 minutes, stirring frequently with a wooden spoon to break up any lumps. Add the onion, garlic, and bell pepper, and cook for 3 minutes, stirring occasionally. Stir in the chili powder and cook for an additional 2 minutes.

2 Stir in the tomato paste, then pour in the chicken stock and season to taste with salt and pepper. Bring to a boil, then reduce the heat and simmer covered for 20 minutes.

3 Add the kidney and chili beans, and cook, stirring occasionally, for 10 minutes or until the chicken is tender.

4 Meanwhile, bring a large pan of lightly salted water to a boil. Add the spaghetti and cook according to the package directions or until al dente.

5 Drain the spaghetti. Arrange on warmed plates, and spoon over the chicken and bean mixture. Serve with the grated cheese, guacamole, and salsa.

INGREDIENTS
Serves 4

2 tbsp. olive oil
1 lb. ground chicken
1 red onion, peeled and chopped
2 garlic cloves, peeled and chopped
1 red bell pepper, deseeded and chopped
1–2 tsp. hot chili powder
2 tbsp. tomato paste
1 cup chicken stock
salt and freshly ground black pepper
15-oz. can red kidney beans, drained
15-oz. can chili beans, drained
12 oz. spaghetti

TO SERVE:
Monterey Jack or cheddar cheese, grated
guacamole
hot chili salsa

Helpful Hint

A variety of chili powders are available. The most common is the red powder made from dried red chilies, which may be mild or hot. A darker powder, which contains a mixture of ground chili and herbs, is specifically for use in Mexican and Southwest dishes.

Pesto Chicken Tagliatelle

1 Heat the oil in a large skillet, then add the chicken and cook for 8 minutes or until golden brown, stirring occasionally. Using a slotted spoon, remove the chicken from the pan, then drain on paper towels and set aside.

2 Melt the butter in the skillet. Add the leeks and cook for 3–5 minutes or until slightly softened, stirring occasionally. Add the oyster and chestnut mushrooms, and cook for 5 minutes or until browned, stirring occasionally.

3 Bring a large pan of lightly salted water to a boil. Add the tagliatelle, then return to a boil and cook for 4 minutes or until al dente.

4 Add the chicken, pesto, and crème fraîche to the mushroom mixture. Stir, then heat through completely. Stir in the grated Parmesan cheese and season to taste with salt and pepper.

5 Drain the tagliatelle thoroughly and pile onto warmed plates. Spoon over the sauce and serve immediately.

INGREDIENTS
Serves 4

2 tbsp. olive oil

12 oz. boneless and skinless chicken breasts, cut into chunks

¾ stick butter

2 medium leeks, trimmed and thinly sliced

1¼ cups oyster mushrooms, trimmed and halved

2¼ cups small open chestnut mushrooms, wiped and halved

1 lb. fresh tagliatelle

4–6 tbsp. red pesto

¾ cup crème fraîche

½ cup freshly grated Parmesan cheese

salt and freshly ground black pepper

Food Fact

Classic pesto is green because it is made from basil. Red pesto is made from a purée of sun-dried tomatoes. Both types of pesto make great pantry standbys since they can be simply tossed with cooked pasta for the speediest of meals. They are even more wonderful livened up with a little crème fraîche, as here, or with mascarpone cheese.

Chicken & Shrimp-Stacked Ravioli

1 Heat the olive oil in a large skillet, then add the onion and garlic and cook for 5 minutes or until softened, stirring occasionally. Add the chicken pieces and fry for 4 minutes or until heated through, turning occasionally.

2 Stir in the chopped tomato, wine, and cream and bring to a boil. Lower the heat and simmer for about 5 minutes or until reduced and thickened. Stir in the shrimp and tarragon, and season to taste with salt and pepper. Heat the sauce through gently.

3 Meanwhile, bring a large pan of lightly salted water to a boil and add 2 lasagna sheets. Return to a boil and cook for 2 minutes, stirring gently to avoid sticking. Remove from the pan using a slotted spoon and keep warm. Repeat with the remaining sheets.

4 Cut each sheet of lasagna in half. Place two pieces on each of the warmed plates and divide half of the chicken mixture among them. Top each serving with a second sheet of lasagna and divide the remainder of the chicken mixture among them. Top with a final layer of lasagna. Garnish with tarragon sprigs and serve immediately.

INGREDIENTS
Serves 4

1 tbsp. olive oil

1 onion, peeled and chopped

1 garlic clove, peeled and chopped

1 lb. boned and skinned cooked chicken, cut into large pieces

1 beefsteak tomato, deseeded and chopped

⅔ cup dry white wine

⅔ cup heavy cream

9 oz. peeled cooked shrimp, thawed if frozen

2 tbsp. freshly chopped tarragon, plus sprigs to garnish

salt and freshly ground black pepper

8 sheets fresh lasagna

Helpful Hint

Always check the package directions when cooking lasagna; some brands may need longer cooking than others. It should be cooked until al dente—tender, but firm to the bite. Dried lasagna—either plain or verde—may be used instead of fresh if preferred, but it will take longer to cook.

Penne with Pan-fried Chicken & Capers

1 Trim the chicken and cut into bite-sized pieces. Season the flour with salt and pepper, then toss the chicken in the seasoned flour and set aside.

2 Bring a large pan of lightly salted water to a rolling boil. Add the penne and cook according to the package directions or until al dente.

3 Meanwhile, heat the oil in a large skillet. Add the chicken and cook for 8 minutes or until golden on all sides, stirring frequently. Transfer the chicken to a plate and set aside.

4 Add the onion and garlic to the oil remaining in the skillet and cook for 5 minutes or until softened, stirring frequently.

5 Return the chicken to the skillet. Stir in the pesto and mascarpone cheese and heat through, stirring gently, until smooth. Stir in the whole-grain mustard, lemon juice, basil, and capers. Season to taste, then continue to heat through until piping hot.

6 Drain the penne thoroughly and return to the pan. Pour over the sauce and toss well to coat. Arrange the pasta on individual warmed plates. Sprinkle the cheese on top and serve immediately.

INGREDIENTS
Serves 4

4 boneless and skinless chicken breasts
2 tbsp. all-purpose flour
salt and freshly ground black pepper
3 cups penne
2 tbsp. olive oil
1 red onion, peeled and sliced
1 garlic clove, peeled and chopped
4–6 tbsp. pesto
1 cup mascarpone cheese
1 tsp. whole-grain mustard
1 tbsp. lemon juice
2 tbsp. freshly chopped basil
3 tbsp. capers in brine, rinsed and drained
freshly shaved Pecorino Romano cheese

Food Fact

Pecorino Romano is a cooked, pressed cheese made in dairies in and around Rome. It is similar to Parmesan (which may be used instead, if preferred) with a dense texture, pale yellow color, and almost smoky aroma. Its flavor is very salty, so take care when seasoning the pasta and chicken when cooking.

Spaghetti with Pesto

1 To make the pesto, place the Parmesan cheese in a food processor with the basil leaves, pine nuts, and garlic, and process until well-blended.

2 With the motor running, gradually pour in the extra-virgin olive oil until a thick sauce forms. Add a little more oil if the sauce seems too thick. Season to taste with salt and pepper. Transfer to a bowl and cover, then store in the refrigerator until required.

3 Bring a large pan of lightly salted water to a rolling boil. Add the spaghetti and cook according to the package directions or until al dente.

4 Drain the spaghetti thoroughly and return to the pan. Stir in the pesto and toss lightly. Heat through gently, then spoon the pasta into a warmed serving dish or onto individual plates. Garnish with basil leaves and serve immediately with extra Parmesan cheese.

INGREDIENTS
Serves 4

1¼ cups freshly grated Parmesan cheese, plus extra to serve

⅓ cup fresh basil leaves, plus extra to garnish

6 tbsp. pine nuts

3 large garlic cloves, peeled

¾ cup extra-virgin olive oil, plus more if necessary

salt and freshly ground pepper

14 oz. spaghetti

Helpful Hint

You can still make pesto if you do not have a food processor. Tear the basil leaves and place them in a mortar with the garlic, pine nuts, and a tablespoonful of the oil. Pound to a paste using a pestle, gradually working in the rest of the oil. Transfer to a bowl and stir in the cheese. Season to taste with salt and pepper. Pesto will keep for 2–3 days if stored in the refrigerator.

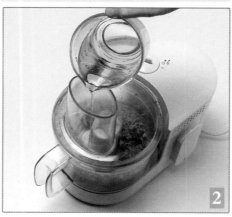

Pasta Shells with Broccoli & Capers

1 Bring a large pan of lightly salted water to a rolling boil. Add the conchiglie, then return to a boil and cook for 2 minutes. Add the broccoli to the pan. Return to a boil and continue cooking for 8–10 minutes or until the conchiglie is al dente.

2 Meanwhile, heat the olive oil in a large skillet, then add the onion and cook for 5 minutes or until softened, stirring frequently. Stir in the capers and chili flakes, and cook for an additional 2 minutes.

3 Drain the pasta and broccoli and add to the skillet. Toss the ingredients to mix thoroughly. Sprinkle over the cheeses, then stir until the cheeses have just melted. Season to taste with salt and pepper, then spoon into a warmed serving dish. Garnish with chopped parsley and serve immediately with extra Parmesan cheese.

INGREDIENTS
Serves 4

3½ cups conchiglie (shells)
1 lb. broccoli florets, cut into small pieces
5 tbsp. olive oil
1 large onion, peeled and finely chopped
4 tbsp. capers in brine, rinsed and drained
½ tsp. dried chili flakes (optional)
¾ cup freshly grated Parmesan cheese, plus extra to serve
¼ cup grated pecorino cheese
salt and freshly ground black pepper
2 tbsp. freshly chopped Italian parsley, to garnish

Helpful Hint

Chili flakes are made from dried, crushed chilies and add a pungent hot spiciness to this dish. There are lots of other chili products that you could use instead. For instance, substitute a tablespoonful of chili oil for one of the tablespoons of olive oil, or add a dash of hot sauce at the end of cooking.

Venetian Herb Orzo

1 Rinse the spinach leaves in cold water several times and set aside. Finely chop the arugula leaves with the parsley and mint. Thinly slice the green of the scallions.

2 Bring a large pan of water to a boil, then add the spinach leaves, herbs, and scallions, and cook for about 10 seconds. Remove and rinse under cold running water. Drain well, and using your hands, squeeze out all the excess moisture.

3 Place the spinach, herbs, and scallions in a food processor. Blend for 1 minute. Then, with the motor running, gradually pour in the olive oil until the sauce is well-blended.

4 Meanwhile, bring a large pan of lightly salted water to a rolling boil. Add the pasta and cook according to the package directions or until al dente. Drain thoroughly and place in a large, warmed bowl.

5 Add the spinach sauce to the orzo and stir lightly until the orzo is well-coated. Stir in an extra tablespoon of olive oil if the mixture seems too thick. Season well with salt and pepper. Serve immediately on warmed plates or let cool to room temperature.

INGREDIENTS
Serves 4–6

2⅓ cups baby spinach leaves
1⅔ cups arugula leaves
⅔ cup Italian parsley
few leaves of fresh mint
6 scallions, trimmed
3 tbsp. extra-virgin olive oil, plus more if required
1 lb. orzo
salt and freshly ground black pepper

Food Fact

Also called "rocket," arugula adds a peppery flavor to many dishes. The tender tiny leaves have the most delicate flavor, and as they grow in size, the flavor becomes more pronounced.

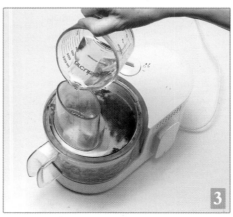

Cheesy Pasta with Tomatoes & Cream

1 Place the ricotta cheese in a bowl and beat until smooth, then add the remaining cheeses with the eggs, herbs, and seasoning to taste. Beat well until creamy and smooth.

2 Cut the prepared pasta dough into quarters. Working with one quarter at a time and covering the remaining quarters with a clean, damp dishtowel, roll out the pasta very thinly. Using a 4-inch pastry cutter or small saucer, cut out as many rounds as possible.

3 Place a small tablespoonful of the filling mixture slightly below the center of each round. Lightly moisten the edge of the round with water and fold in half to form a filled half-moon shape. Using a dinner fork, press the edges together firmly.

4 Transfer to a lightly floured cookie sheet and continue filling the remaining pasta. Leave to dry for 15 minutes.

5 Heat the oil in a large pan, then add the onions and cook for 3–4 minutes or until beginning to soften. Add the garlic and cook for 1–2 minutes, then add the tomatoes, vermouth, and cream, and bring to a boil. Simmer for 10–15 minutes or until thickened and reduced.

6 Bring a large pan of salted water to a boil. Add the filled pasta and return to a boil. Cook, stirring frequently to prevent sticking, for 5 minutes or until al dente. Drain and return to the pan. Pour over the tomato and cream sauce. Garnish with basil leaves and serve immediately.

INGREDIENTS
Serves 4

Fresh pasta (see Fresh Tagliatelle with Zucchini, page 16)
1 cup fresh ricotta cheese
2 cups grated, smoked mozzarella (use normal if smoked is unavailable)
1 cup freshly grated pecorino or Parmesan cheese
2 medium eggs, lightly beaten
2–3 tbsp. finely chopped mint, basil, or parsley
salt and freshly ground black pepper

FOR THE SAUCE:

2 tbsp. olive oil
1 small onion, peeled and finely chopped
2 garlic cloves, peeled and finely chopped
1 lb. ripe plum tomatoes, peeled, deseeded, and finely chopped
¼ cup white vermouth
1 cup heavy cream
fresh basil leaves, to garnish

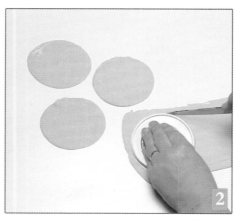

Pasta-Stuffed Bell Peppers

1 Preheat the oven to 375° F. Bring a pan of water to a boil. Trim the bottom of each bell pepper so it sits straight. Blanch the bell peppers for 2–3 minutes, then drain on paper towels.

2 Return the water to a boil. Add ½ teaspoon of salt and the pasta, and cook for 3–4 minutes or until al dente. Drain thoroughly, saving the water. Rinse under cold running water, then drain again and set aside.

3 Heat 2 tablespoons of the olive oil in a large skillet, then add the onion and cook for 3–4 minutes. Add the garlic and cook for 1 minute. Stir in the tomatoes and wine, and cook for

5 minutes, stirring frequently. Add the olives, herbs, mozzarella cheese, and half the Parmesan cheese. Season to taste with salt and pepper. Remove from the heat and stir in the pasta.

4 Dry the insides of the bell peppers with paper towels, then season lightly. Arrange the bell peppers in a lightly greased, shallow baking dish and fill with the pasta mixture. Sprinkle with the remaining Parmesan cheese and drizzle the remaining oil over the peppers. Pour in boiling water to ½ inch up the sides of the dish. Cook in the preheated oven for 25 minutes or until cooked. Serve immediately with freshly made tomato sauce.

INGREDIENTS
Serves 6

6 red, yellow, or orange bell peppers, tops cut off and deseeded
salt and freshly ground black pepper
1½ cups tiny pasta shapes
4 tbsp. olive oil
1 onion, peeled and finely chopped
2 garlic cloves, peeled and finely chopped
3 ripe plum tomatoes, skinned, deseeded, and chopped
¼ cup dry white wine
8 pitted black olives, chopped
4 tbsp. freshly chopped mixed herbs, such as parsley, basil, oregano, or marjoram
1 cup diced mozzarella cheese
4 tbsp. grated Parmesan cheese
fresh tomato sauce, preferably homemade, to serve

Tasty Tip

For a rich tomato sauce, chop 2 lbs. ripe tomatoes, then place in a pan with 1 crushed garlic clove, 1 tablespoon olive oil, and 2 tablespoons Worcestershire sauce. Cook until soft. Sieve or purée and serve with the bell peppers.

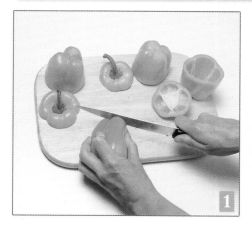

Fusilli with Zucchini & Sun-Dried Tomatoes

1 Heat 2 tablespoons of the olive oil in a large skillet, then add the onion and cook for 5-7 minutes or until softened. Add the chopped garlic and zucchini slices, and cook for an additional 5 minutes, stirring occasionally.

2 Stir the chopped tomatoes and the sun-dried tomatoes into the skillet, and season to taste with salt and pepper. Cook until the zucchini are just tender and the sauce is slightly thickened.

3 Bring a large pan of lightly salted water to a rolling boil. Add the fusilli and cook according to the package directions or until al dente.

4 Drain the fusilli thoroughly and return to the pan. Add the butter and remaining oil, and toss to coat. Stir the chopped basil or parsley into the zucchini mixture and pour over the fusilli. Toss and spoon into a warmed serving dish. Serve with grated Parmesan or pecorino cheese.

INGREDIENTS
Serves 6

5 tbsp. olive oil

1 large onion, peeled and thinly sliced

2 garlic cloves, peeled and finely chopped

1½ lbs. zucchini, trimmed and sliced

14-oz. can chopped plum tomatoes

12 sun-dried tomatoes, cut into thin strips

salt and freshly ground black pepper

4 cups fusilli

2 tbsp. butter, diced

2 tbsp. freshly chopped basil or Italian parsley

grated Parmesan or pecorino cheese, for serving

Food Fact

Sun-dried tomatoes come in jars with olive oil or simply dried in packages, in which case they will need rehydrating. The latter are better for this recipe, as they will soak up the juices from the chopped tomatoes and zucchini and help to thicken the sauce.

Linguine with Walnut Pesto

INGREDIENTS
Serves 4

1 cup walnut halves

1–2 garlic cloves, peeled and
   coarsely chopped

⅓ cup dried bread crumbs

3 tbsp. extra-virgin olive oil

1 tbsp. walnut oil

3–4 tbsp. freshly chopped parsley

½ stick butter, softened

2 tbsp. heavy cream

¼ cup grated Parmesan cheese,
   plus extra to serve

salt and freshly ground black
   pepper

1 lb. linguine

1 Bring a pan of water to a boil. Add the walnut halves and simmer for about 1 minute. Drain and turn onto a clean dishtowel. Using the towel, rub the nuts gently to loosen the skins, then turn into a coarse sieve or colander and shake to separate the skins. Discard the skins and coarsely chop the nuts.

2 With the the food processor running, drop in the garlic cloves and chop finely. Remove the lid, then add the walnuts, bread crumbs, olive and walnut oils, and the parsley. Blend to a paste with a crumbly texture.

3 Scrape the nut mixture into a bowl, then add the softened butter and, using a wooden spoon, cream them together. Gradually beat in the cream and the Parmesan cheese. Season the walnut pesto to taste with salt and pepper.

4 Bring a large pan of lightly salted water to a rolling boil. Add the linguine and cook according to the package instructions or until al dente.

5 Drain the linguine thoroughly, setting aside 1–2 tablespoons of the cooking water. Return the linguine and water to the pan. Add the walnut pesto, 1 tablespoon at a time, tossing and stirring until well-coated. Tip into a warmed serving dish or spoon onto individual plates. Serve immediately with the extra grated Parmesan cheese.

Helpful Hint

It is important to use dried bread crumbs for this recipe. Avoid the bright orange variety, which are unsuitable. Spread about 1 cup fresh bread crumbs on a cookie sheet and bake in a very low oven for about 20–25 minutes, stirring occasionally, until dry but not colored.

Four-Cheese Tagliatelle

1 Place the whipping cream with the garlic cloves in a medium pan, and heat gently until small bubbles begin to form around the edge of the pan. Using a slotted spoon, remove and discard the garlic cloves.

2 Add all the cheeses to the pan and stir until melted. Season with a little salt and a lot of black pepper. Keep the sauce warm over a low heat, but do not let it come to a boil.

3 Meanwhile, bring a large pan of lightly salted water to a boil. Add the tagliatelle, then return to a boil and cook for 2–3 minutes or until al dente.

4 Drain the pasta and return it to the pan. Pour the sauce over the pasta, then add the chives and toss lightly until well-coated. Spoon into a warmed serving dish or spoon onto individual plates. Garnish with a few basil leaves and serve immediately with extra Parmesan cheese.

INGREDIENTS
Serves 4

1¼ cups whipping cream
4 garlic cloves, peeled and lightly bruised
¾ cup diced fontina cheese
¾ cup grated Gruyère cheese
¾ cup diced mozzarella cheese
¼ cup grated Parmesan cheese, plus extra to serve
salt and freshly ground black pepper
10 oz. fresh green tagliatelle
1–2 tbsp. freshly cut chives
fresh basil leaves, to garnish

Helpful Hint

Fresh pasta takes much less time to cook than dried pasta and 2–3 minutes is usually long enough for it to be al dente, but check the package for cooking directions. Tagliatelle comes from Bologna, where it is usually served with a meat sauce. Green tagliatelle is generally flavored with spinach, but it is also available flavored with fresh herbs, which would go particularly well with the rich cheese sauce in this recipe.

Spaghetti alla Puttanesca

1 Heat the olive oil in a large skillet, then add the anchovies and cook, stirring with a wooden spoon and crushing the anchovies until they disintegrate. Add the garlic and dried chilies, and cook for 1 minute, stirring frequently.

2 Add the tomatoes, olives, capers, oregano, and tomato paste, and cook, stirring occasionally, for 15 minutes or until the liquid has evaporated and the sauce is thickened. Season the tomato sauce to taste with salt and pepper.

3 Meanwhile, bring a large pan of lightly salted water to a boil. Add the spaghetti and cook according to the package directions or until al dente.

4 Drain the spaghetti thoroughly, setting aside 1–2 tablespoons of the the cooking water. Return the spaghetti with the reserved water to the pan. Pour the tomato sauce over the spaghetti, then add the chopped parsley and toss to coat. Spoon into a warmed serving dish or onto individual plates and serve immediately.

INGREDIENTS
Serves 4

4 tbsp. olive oil

2 oz. anchovy fillets in olive oil, drained and coarsely chopped

2 garlic cloves, peeled and finely chopped

½ tsp. crushed dried chilies

14-oz. can chopped plum tomatoes

1 cup pitted black olives, cut in half

2 tbsp. capers, rinsed and drained

1 tsp. freshly chopped oregano

1 tbsp. tomato paste

salt and freshly ground black pepper

14 oz. spaghetti

2 tbsp. freshly chopped parsley

Helpful Hint

Anchovies are heavily salted after filleting to preserve them, so should be used only in small quantities. For a less-salty dish, drain them and soak in a little milk for about 20 minutes before using. You can, of course, omit the anchovies to make a vegetarian version of this recipe.

Tagliatelle Primavera

1 Bring a medium pan of salted water to a boil. Add the asparagus and blanch for 1–2 minutes or until just beginning to soften. Using a slotted spoon, transfer to a colander and rinse under cold running water. Repeat with the carrots and zucchini. Add the snow peas and return to a boil, then drain, rinse immediately, and drain again. Set aside the blanched vegetables.

2 Heat the butter in a large skillet. Add the onion and red bell pepper and cook for 5 minutes or until they begin to soften and color. Pour in the dry vermouth; it will bubble, steam, and evaporate almost immediately. Stir in the cream and simmer over a medium-low heat until reduced by about half. Add the blanched vegetables with the leeks, peas, and seasoning, and heat through for 2 minutes.

3 Meanwhile, bring a large pan of lightly salted water to a boil, then add the tagliatelle and return to a boil. Cook for 2-3 minutes or until al dente. Drain and return to the pan.

4 Stir the chopped parsley into the cream and vegetable sauce, then pour over the pasta and toss to coat thoroughly. Sprinkle with the grated Parmesan cheese and toss lightly. Spoon into a warmed serving bowl or spoon onto individual plates and serve immediately.

INGREDIENTS
Serves 4

4 oz. asparagus, lightly peeled and cut into 2½ in. lengths

2 carrots, peeled and cut into julienne strips

2 zucchini, trimmed and cut into julienne strips

⅓ cup small snow peas

½ cup butter

1 small onion, peeled and finely chopped

1 small red bell pepper, deseeded and finely chopped

¼ cup dry vermouth

1 cup heavy cream

1 small leek, trimmed and julienned

¾ cup fresh green peas (or frozen, thawed)

salt and freshly ground black pepper

14 oz. fresh tagliatelle

2 tbsp. freshly chopped Italian parsley

¼ cup grated Parmesan cheese

Helpful Hint

If using thin asparagus spears, there is no need to peel the stems. This is only necessary on the long spears that can have a woody stalk as the season progresses.

Eggplant & Ravioli Parmigiana

1 Preheat the oven to 350° F. Heat 2 tablespoons of the olive oil in a large, heavy-based pan, then add the onion and cook for 6–7 minutes or until softened. Add the garlic, then cook for 1 minute. Stir in the tomatoes, sugar, bay leaf, dried oregano, and basil, then bring to a boil, stirring frequently. Simmer for 30–35 minutes or until thickened and reduced, stirring occasionally. Stir in the fresh basil and season to taste with salt and pepper. Remove the tomato sauce from the heat and set aside.

2 Heat the remaining olive oil in a large, heavy-based skillet over a high heat. Dip the eggplant slices in the egg mixture, then in the bread crumbs. Cook in batches until golden on both sides. Drain on paper towels. Add more oil between batches if necessary.

3 Spoon a little tomato sauce into the base of a lightly greased large baking dish. Cover with a layer of eggplant slices, a sprinkling of Parmesan cheese, a layer of mozzarella cheese, then more sauce. Repeat the layers, then cover the sauce with a layer of cooked ravioli. Continue to layer in this way, ending with a layer of mozzarella cheese. Sprinkle the top with Parmesan cheese.

4 Drizzle with a little extra olive oil if desired, then bake in the preheated oven for 30 minutes or until golden brown and bubbling. Serve immediately.

INGREDIENTS
Serves 6

4 tbsp. olive oil

1 large onion, peeled and finely chopped

2–3 garlic cloves, peeled and crushed

2 14-oz. cans chopped tomatoes

2 tsp. brown sugar

1 dried bay leaf

1 tsp. dried oregano

1 tsp. dried basil

2 tbsp. freshly shredded basil

salt and freshly ground black pepper

2–3 medium eggplants, sliced crosswise ½ in. thick

2 medium eggs, beaten with 1 tbsp. water

1 cup dried bread crumbs

3/4 cup freshly grated Parmesan cheese

14 oz. mozzarella cheese, thinly sliced

9 oz. cheese-filled ravioli, cooked and drained

Helpful Hint

Eggplants absorb a huge amount of oil during cooking, so use a good nonstick skillet and gradually add oil as required. You can use baby eggplants for this recipe if you prefer. Trim off the stalk ends, then cut them lengthwise into ½-inch strips.

Zucchini Lasagna

1 Preheat the oven to 400° F. Heat the oil in a large skillet, then add the onion and cook for 3–5 minutes. Add the mushrooms and cook for 2 minutes. Add the zucchini and cook for an additional 3–4 minutes, or until tender. Stir in the garlic, thyme, and basil or parsley, then season to taste with salt and pepper. Remove from the heat and set aside.

2 Spoon one third of the white sauce onto the base of a lightly greased large baking dish. Arrange a layer of lasagna over the sauce. Spread half the zucchini mixture over the pasta, then sprinkle with some of the mozzarella and some of the Parmesan cheese. Repeat with more white sauce and another layer of lasagna, then cover with half the drained tomatoes.

3 Cover the tomatoes with lasagna, the remaining zucchini mixture, and some mozzarella and Parmesan cheese. Repeat the layers, ending with a layer of lasagna sheets, white sauce, and the remaining Parmesan cheese. Bake in the preheated oven for 35 minutes or until golden. Serve immediately.

INGREDIENTS
Serves 8

2 tbsp. olive oil

1 medium onion, peeled and finely chopped

4 cups mushrooms, wiped and thinly sliced

3–4 zucchini, trimmed and thinly sliced

2 garlic cloves, peeled and finely chopped

½ tsp. dried thyme

1–2 tbsp. freshly chopped basil or Italian parsley

salt and freshly ground black pepper

1 quantity prepared white sauce, (see page 98)

12 oz. lasagna sheets, cooked

2 cups grated mozzarella cheese

½ cup grated Parmesan cheese

14-oz. canned chopped tomatoes, drained

Helpful Hint

There is now a huge range of canned tomatoes available. Look for canned cherry tomatoes, which have a much sweeter flavor, or those with added ingredients and flavorings. Tomatoes with chopped bell peppers, garlic, or fresh herbs would all work well here and add extra flavor.

Baked Macaroni and Cheese

1 Preheat the oven to 375 °F. Bring a large heavy-based pan of lightly salted water to a rolling boil. Add the macaroni and cook according to the package directions or until al dente. Drain the pasta thoroughly and set aside.

2 Meanwhile, melt ½ cup of the butter in a large, heavy-based pan, then add the onion and cook, stirring frequently, for 5–7 minutes or until softened. Sprinkle in the flour and cook, stirring constantly, for about 2 minutes. Remove the pan from the heat and stir in the milk, then return to the heat and cook, stirring, until a smooth sauce has formed.

3 Add the bay leaf and thyme to the sauce, and season to taste with salt, pepper, cayenne pepper, and freshly grated nutmeg. Simmer for about 15 minutes, stirring frequently, until thickened and smooth.

4 Remove the sauce from the heat. Add the leeks, mustard, and cheddar cheese, and stir until the cheese has melted. Stir in the macaroni, then spoon into a lightly greased baking dish.

5 Sprinkle the bread crumbs and Parmesan cheese over the macaroni. Dot with the remaining butter, then bake in the preheated oven for 1 hour or until golden. Garnish with a basil sprig and serve immediately.

INGREDIENTS
Serves 8

4 cups macaroni
¾ cup butter
1 onion, peeled and finely chopped
3 tbsp. all-purpose flour
4 cups milk
1–2 dried bay leaves
½ tsp. dried thyme
salt and freshly ground black pepper
cayenne pepper
freshly grated nutmeg
2 small leeks, trimmed, finely chopped, cooked, and drained
1 tbsp. Dijon mustard
3½ cups grated cheddar cheese
2 tbsp. dried bread crumbs
2 tbsp. freshly grated Parmesan cheese
basil sprig, to garnish

Helpful Hint

Make sure that you simmer the macaroni only until just al dente and drain immediately, as it will continue to cook in the oven, where it needs to soak up the flavors of the sauce. For a more substantial dish, stir some chopped, lean smoked bacon into the macaroni before baking.

Penne with Vodka & Caviar

1 Bring a large pan of lightly salted water to a rolling boil. Add the penne and cook according to the package directions or until al dente. Drain thoroughly and set aside.

2 Heat the butter in a large skillet or wok, then add the scallions and stir-fry for 1 minute. Stir in the garlic and cook for an additional minute. Pour the vodka into the pan; it will bubble and steam. Cook until the vodka is reduced by about half, then add the heavy cream and return to a boil. Simmer gently for 2–3 minutes or until the sauce has thickened slightly.

3 Stir in the tomatoes, then stir in all but 1 tablespoon of the caviar and season to taste with salt and pepper. Add the penne and toss lightly to coat. Cook for 1 minute or until heated through. Divide the mixture among four warmed pasta bowls and garnish with the remaining caviar. Serve immediately.

INGREDIENTS
Serves 4

3½ cups penne

2 tbsp. butter

4–6 scallions, trimmed and thinly sliced

1 garlic clove, peeled and finely chopped

½ cup vodka

¾ cup heavy cream

1–2 ripe plum tomatoes, skinned, deseeded, and chopped

3 oz. caviar

salt and freshly ground black pepper

Food Fact

Authentic sturgeon caviar is very expensive. Red caviar from salmon, or black or red lumpfish roe, can be substituted. Alternatively, 6 oz. of thinly sliced smoked salmon pieces can also be substituted. Sturgeon caviar has a salty flavor, so always check the taste before adding salt. Smoked salmon and lumpfish roe have a much saltier taste, however, so no additional salt would be necessary.

Rigatoni with Gorgonzola & Walnuts

1 Bring a large pan of lightly salted water to a rolling boil. Add the rigatoni and cook according to the package directions or until al dente. Drain the pasta thoroughly, then set aside and keep warm.

2 Melt the butter in a large pan or wok over a medium heat. Add the Gorgonzola cheese and stir until just melted. Add the brandy (if desired) and cook for 30 seconds, then pour in the whipping or heavy cream and cook for 1–2 minutes, stirring until the sauce is smooth.

3 Stir in the walnut pieces, basil, and half the Parmesan cheese, then add the rigatoni. Season with salt and pepper. Return to the heat, stirring frequently, until heated through. Divide the pasta among four warmed bowls, then sprinkle with the remaining Parmesan cheese and serve immediately with cherry tomatoes and fresh green salad leaves.

INGREDIENTS
Serves 4

3½ cups rigatoni
½ stick butter
1 cup crumbled Gorgonzola cheese
2 tbsp. brandy, optional
¾ cup whipping or heavy cream
½ cup walnut pieces, lightly toasted and coarsely chopped
1 tbsp. freshly chopped basil
½ cup freshly grated Parmesan cheese
salt and freshly ground black pepper

TO SERVE:
cherry tomatoes
fresh green salad leaves

Tasty Tip

This blue cheese sauce is also very good with pappardelle or lasagnette, both very wide egg pasta noodles. Either whipping or heavy cream may be used here; heavy cream is higher in fat, so will give a richer, creamier finish to the sauce. If preferred, you could use sour cream, but it must be heated gently since it can curdle at high temperatures.

Pumpkin-Filled Pasta with Butter & Sage

1 Mix together the ingredients for the filling in a bowl, seasoning to taste with freshly grated nutmeg, salt, and pepper. If the mixture seems too wet, add a few more bread crumbs to bind.

2 Cut the pasta dough into quarters. Work with one quarter at a time, covering the remaining quarters with a damp dishtowel. Roll out the dough very thinly into a strip 4 inches wide. Drop spoonfuls of the filling along the strip 2½ inches apart, in two rows about 2 inches apart. Moisten the outside edges and the spaces between the filling with water.

3 Roll out another strip of pasta and lay it over the filled strip. Press down gently along both edges and between

the filled sections. Using a fluted pastry wheel, cut along both long sides, down the center, and between the fillings to form cushions. Transfer the cushions to a lightly floured cookie sheet. Continue making cushions and let dry for 30 minutes.

4 Bring a large pan of lightly salted water to a boil. Add the pasta cushions and return to a boil. Cook, stirring frequently, for 4–5 minutes or until al dente. Drain carefully.

5 Heat the butter in a pan, then stir in the shredded sage leaves and cook for 30 seconds. Add the pasta cushions and stir gently, then spoon into serving bowls. Sprinkle with the grated Parmesan cheese and serve immediately.

INGREDIENTS
Serves 6–8

1 quantity fresh pasta dough (see page 16)
1 cup butter
2 tbsp. freshly shredded sage leaves
½ cup freshly grated Parmesan cheese, to serve

FOR THE FILLING:

about 1 cup freshly cooked pumpkin or sweet potato flesh, mashed and cooled
⅓ cup dried bread crumbs
1 cup freshly grated Parmesan cheese
1 medium egg yolk
½ tsp. soft brown sugar
2 tbsp. freshly chopped parsley
freshly grated nutmeg
salt and freshly ground black pepper

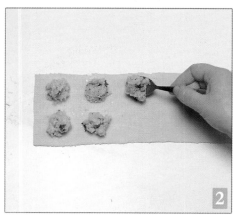

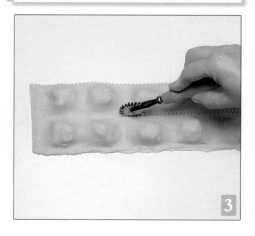

Cold Sesame Noodles

1 Bring a large pan of lightly salted water to a rolling boil. Add the noodles or spaghetti and cook according to the package directions or until al dente. Drain. Rinse and drain again, then toss in the sesame oil and set aside.

2 Heat the peanut oil in a wok or large skillet over a high heat. Add the green bell pepper, daikon, and snow peas or green beans, and stir-fry for 1 minute. Stir in the garlic and cook for 30 seconds.

3 Add the soy sauce to the pan with the vinegar, chili

sauce, sugar, peanut butter, and ¼ cup of hot water. Simmer, stirring constantly, until the peanut butter is smooth, adding a little more water if necessary and adjusting the seasoning to taste.

4 Add the scallions and the noodles or spaghetti to the peanut sauce and cook, stirring, for 2–3 minutes or until heated through. Spoon the mixture into a large serving bowl and leave to cool to room temperature, stirring occasionally. Garnish with the toasted sesame seeds and cucumber julienne strips before serving.

INGREDIENTS
Serves 4–8

1 lb. buckwheat (soba) noodles or whole-wheat spaghetti
salt
1 tbsp. sesame oil
1 tbsp. peanut oil
1 green bell pepper, deseeded and thinly sliced
4 oz. daikon, julienned
¾ cup trimmed and sliced snow peas or green beans
2 garlic cloves, peeled and finely chopped
2 tbsp. soy sauce, or to taste
1 tbsp. cider vinegar
2 tbsp. sweet chili sauce, or to taste
2 tsp. sugar
⅓ cup peanut butter
6–8 scallions, trimmed and diagonally sliced

GARNISH:
toasted sesame seeds
julienned strips of cucumber

Food Fact

Daikon, also known as "Japanese radish," resembles a white carrot in shape. It has a very fresh, peppery flavor and is often used in salads, either peeled or grated. Because it has a high water content, it should be sprinkled with salt and drained in a sieve over a bowl for about 30 minutes after preparing. Rinse well under cold running water and pat dry on paper towels before stir-frying.

Singapore Noodles

1 Bring a large pan of lightly salted water to a rolling boil. Add the noodles and cook according to the package directions or until al dente. Drain thoroughly and toss with 1 tablespoon of the oil.

2 Heat the remaining oil in a wok or large skillet over high heat. Add the mushrooms, ginger, chili, and red bell pepper, and stir-fry for 2 minutes. Add the garlic, zucchini, scallions, and garden peas, and stir lightly.

3 Push the vegetables to one side and add the curry paste, ketchup, and about ½ cup hot water. Season to taste with salt or a few drops of soy sauce and let boil vigorously, stirring until the paste is smooth.

4 Stir the egg noodles and the bean sprouts into the vegetable mixture, and stir-fry until coated with the paste and completely heated through. Season with more soy sauce if necessary, then turn into a large warmed serving bowl or spoon onto individual plates. Garnish the noodles with sesame seeds and cilantro leaves. Serve immediately.

INGREDIENTS
Serves 4

8 oz. thin, round egg noodles

3 tbsp. peanut or vegetable oil

2 cups field mushrooms, thinly sliced

1-in. piece ginger, peeled and finely chopped

1 red chili, deseeded and thinly sliced

1 red bell pepper, deseeded and thinly sliced

2 garlic cloves, peeled and crushed

1 medium zucchini, cut in half lengthwise and diagonally sliced

4–6 scallions, trimmed and thinly sliced

½ cup frozen garden peas, thawed

1 tbsp. curry paste

2 tbsp. ketchup

salt or soy sauce

1 cup bean sprouts, rinsed and drained

TO GARNISH:

sesame seeds

fresh cilantro leaves

Helpful Hint

There is a huge range of curry pastes available, varying from very mild to extremely hot. Obviously, the choice here depends very much on your personal preference, but try to select one with Asian rather than Indian overtones— Thai green or red curry paste would be a good choice.

Tortellini, Cherry Tomato, & Mozzarella Skewers

1 Preheat the broiler and line a broiler pan with foil, just before cooking. Bring a large pan of lightly salted water to a rolling boil. Add the tortellini and cook according to the package directions or until al dente. Drain and rinse under cold running water. Drain again and toss with 2 tablespoons of the olive oil and set aside.

2 Pour the remaining olive oil into a small bowl. Add the crushed garlic and thyme or basil, then blend well. Season to taste with salt and black pepper and set aside.

3 To assemble the skewers, thread the tortellini alternately with the cherry tomatoes and cubes of mozzarella. Arrange the skewers on the broiler pan and brush generously on all sides with the olive oil mixture.

4 Cook the skewers under the preheated broiler for about 5 minutes or until they begin to turn golden, turning them halfway through cooking. Arrange 2 skewers on each plate and garnish with a few basil leaves. Serve immediately with dressed lettuce leaves.

INGREDIENTS
Serves 6

9 oz. mixed green and plain cheese- or vegetable-filled fresh tortellini
⅔ cup extra-virgin olive oil
2 garlic cloves, peeled and crushed
pinch dried thyme or basil
salt and freshly ground black pepper
8 oz. cherry tomatoes
1 lb. mozzarella, cut into 1-in. cubes
basil leaves, to garnish
dressed lettuce leaves, to serve

Helpful Hint

These skewers make an ideal starter for a barbecue. Alternatively, a small quantity of the prepared ingredients can be threaded onto smaller skewers and served as canapés. If using wooden skewers for this recipe, soak them in cold water for at least 30 minutes before cooking to keep them from scorching under the broiler. The tips of the skewers may be protected with small pieces of foil.

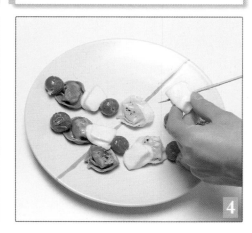

Tortellini & Summer Vegetable Salad

1 Bring a large pan of lightly salted water to a rolling boil. Add the tortellini and cook according to the package directions or until al dente.

2 Using a large slotted spoon, transfer the tortellini to a colander to drain. Rinse under cold running water and drain again. Transfer to a large bowl and toss with 2 tablespoons of the olive oil.

3 Return the pasta water to a boil and drop in the green beans and broccoli florets; blanch them for 2 minutes or until just beginning to soften. Drain, then rinse under cold running water

and drain again thoroughly. Add the vegetables to the tortellini.

4 Add the bell pepper, onion, artichoke hearts, capers, and olives to the bowl; stir lightly.

5 Whisk together the vinegar, mustard, and brown sugar in a bowl, and season to taste with salt and pepper. Slowly whisk in the remaining olive oil to form a thick, creamy dressing. Pour over the tortellini and vegetables, add the chopped basil or parsley, and stir until lightly coated. Transfer to a shallow serving dish or salad bowl. Garnish with the hard-boiled egg quarters and serve.

Food Fact

Black olives are picked when fully ripe and a brownish pink color, then fermented and oxidized until they become black. Dry-cured black olives can be bought from Italian food shops or the delicatessen counter of some large supermarkets, but if you are unable to get them, use ordinary small black olives instead.

INGREDIENTS
Serves 6

12 oz. mixed green and plain cheese-filled fresh tortellini
⅔ cup extra-virgin olive oil
1½ cups trimmed fine green beans
6 oz. broccoli florets
1 yellow or red bell pepper, deseeded and thinly sliced
1 red onion, peeled and sliced
6 oz. jar marinated artichoke hearts, drained and halved
2 tbsp. capers
½ cup dry-cured pitted black olives
3 tbsp. raspberry or balsamic vinegar
1 tbsp. Dijon mustard
1 tsp. soft brown sugar
salt and freshly ground black pepper
2 tbsp. freshly chopped basil or Italian parsley
2 quartered hard-boiled eggs, to garnish

Fettuccine with Calf's Liver & Calvados

1 Season the flour with the salt, black pepper, and paprika, then toss the liver in the flour until well-coated.

2 Melt half the butter and 1 tablespoon of the olive oil in a large skillet and fry the liver in batches for 1 minute or until just browned but still slightly pink inside. Remove using a slotted spoon and place in a warmed dish.

3 Add the remaining butter to the pan. Stir in 1 tablespoon of the seasoned flour and cook for 1 minute. Pour in the Calvados and cider, and cook over a high heat for 30 seconds. Stir the cream into the sauce and simmer for 1 minute to thicken slightly, then season to taste. Return the liver to the pan and heat through.

4 Bring a large pan of lightly salted water to a rolling boil. Add the fettuccine and cook according to the package directions, about 3–4 minutes or until al dente.

5 Drain the fettuccine thoroughly, then return to the pan and toss in the remaining olive oil. Divide among four warmed plates, and spoon the liver and sauce over the pasta. Garnish with thyme sprigs and serve immediately.

INGREDIENTS
Serves 4

½ cup all-purpose flour
salt and freshly ground black pepper
1 tsp. paprika
1 lb. calf's liver, trimmed and thinly sliced
½ stick butter
1½ tbsp. olive oil
2 tbsp. Calvados
⅔ cup cider
⅔ cup whipping cream
12 oz. fresh fettuccine
fresh thyme sprigs, to garnish

Helpful Hint

Calvados is made from apples and adds a fruity taste to this dish, although you can, of course, use ordinary brandy instead. Calf's liver is very tender with a delicate flavor. It should be cooked over a high heat until the outside is brown and crusty and the center still slightly pink. Take care not to overcook the liver, or you will spoil its taste and texture.

Tagliatelle with Stuffed Pork Escalopes

1 Preheat the oven to 350° F. Mix the broccoli with the mozzarella cheese, garlic, and beaten eggs. Season to taste with salt and pepper, and set aside until needed.

2 Using a meat mallet or rolling pin, pound the escalopes on a sheet of waxed paper until ¼ inch thick. Divide the broccoli mixture between the escalopes, and roll each one up from the shortest side. Place the pork rolls in a lightly greased ovenproof dish, then drizzle the olive oil over the rolls and bake in the preheated oven for 40–50 minutes, or until cooked.

3 Meanwhile, melt the butter in a heavy-based pan, then stir in the flour and cook for 2 minutes. Remove from the heat and whisk in the milk and stock. Season to taste, then stir in the mustard and cook until smooth and thickened. Keep warm.

4 Bring a large pan of lightly salted water to a rolling boil. Add the tagliatelle and cook according to the package directions, about 3–4 minutes or until al dente. Drain thoroughly and spoon into a warmed serving dish. Slice each pork roll into 3, place on top of the pasta, and pour the sauce over. Garnish with sage leaves and serve immediately.

INGREDIENTS
Serves 4

¾ cup broccoli florets, finely chopped and blanched
1 cup grated mozzarella cheese
1 garlic clove, peeled and crushed
2 large eggs, beaten
salt and freshly ground black pepper
4 thin pork escalopes, weighing about 3½ oz. each
1 tbsp. olive oil
2 tbsp. butter
2 tbsp. flour
⅔ cup milk
⅔ cup chicken stock
1 tbsp. Dijon mustard
8 oz. fresh tagliatelle
sage leaves, to garnish

Helpful Hint

Pounding the pork escalopes makes them thinner, but tenderizes the meat. Brush with a little oil to keep them from sticking to the mallet or rolling pin, or pound (with the blunt side of the mallet) between two sheets of greased waxed paper or plastic wrap. Take care not to tear the fibers.

Spicy Chicken with Open Ravioli & Tomato Sauce

1 Heat the oil in a skillet, add the onion, and cook gently for 2–3 minutes. Add the cumin, paprika, and cinnamon, and cook for an additional minute. Add the chicken, season to taste with salt and pepper, and cook for 3–4 minutes or until tender. Add the peanut butter and stir well. Set aside.

2 Melt the butter in the skillet, then add the shallot and cook for 2 minutes. Add the tomatoes and garlic, and season to taste. Simmer gently for 20 minutes, or until thickened, then keep the sauce warm.

3 Cut each sheet of lasagna into 6 squares. Bring a large pan of lightly salted water to a rolling boil. Add the lasagna squares, and cook according to the package directions, about 3–4 minutes or until al dente. Drain the lasagna pieces thoroughly, then set aside and keep warm.

4 Layer the pasta squares with the spicy filling on individual warmed plates. Pour over a little of the hot tomato sauce and sprinkle with chopped cilantro. Serve immediately.

INGREDIENTS
Serves 2–3

2 tbsp. olive oil

1 onion, peeled and finely chopped

1 tsp. ground cumin

1 tsp. hot paprika

1 tsp. ground cinnamon

⅔ cup chopped boneless and skinless chicken breasts

salt and freshly ground black pepper

1 tbsp. smooth peanut butter

½ stick butter

1 shallot, peeled and finely chopped

14-oz. can chopped tomatoes

2 garlic cloves, peeled and crushed

4 oz. fresh egg lasagna

2 tbsp. freshly chopped cilantro

Helpful Hint

Remember that fresh pasta should be exactly that; buy no more than two days ahead and preferably on the day that you plan to cook it. Since it contains fresh eggs, it should always be stored in the refrigerator, kept in its package or wrapped in nonstick baking parchment, then in plastic wrap.

Farfalle & Chicken in White Wine Sauce

1 Place the chicken breasts between two sheets of waxed paper and, using a meat mallet or wooden rolling pin, pound as thinly as possible. Season with salt and pepper and set aside.

2 Mash the feta cheese with a fork and blend with the egg and half the tarragon. Divide the mixture between the chicken breasts and roll up each piece. Secure with toothpicks.

3 Heat half the butter and all the olive oil in a skillet, then add the onion and cook for 2–3 minutes. Remove, using a slotted spoon, and set aside. Add the chicken to the skillet and cook for 3–4 minutes or until browned.

4 Pour in the wine and stock, and stir in the remaining tarragon. Cover and simmer gently for 10–15 minutes or until the chicken is cooked.

5 Meanwhile, bring a large pan of lightly salted water to a rolling boil. Add the farfalle and cook according to the package directions, about 3–4 minutes or until al dente. Drain, then toss in the remaining butter and tip into a warm serving dish.

6 Cut each chicken roll into four slices and place on the pasta. Whisk the sauce until smooth, then stir in the sour cream and onions. Heat the sauce gently, then pour over the chicken. Sprinkle with the parsley and serve immediately.

INGREDIENTS
Serves 4

4 boneless and skinless chicken breasts, about 1 lb. in total weight
salt and freshly ground black pepper
4 oz. feta cheese
1 small egg, beaten
2 tbsp. freshly chopped tarragon
½ stick butter
1 tbsp. olive oil
1 onion, peeled and sliced into rings
⅔ cup white wine
⅔ cup chicken stock
12 oz. fresh farfalle
3–4 tbsp. sour cream
2 tbsp. freshly chopped parsley

Food Fact

Feta is a Greek cheese, traditionally made from ewe's milk, but now more often from cow's milk. It is preserved in brine, which gives it a salty flavor; always drain feta before using.

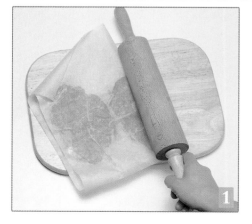

Polenta Roulade with Mozzarella & Spinach

1 Preheat the oven to 475 °F. Oil and line a large jelly roll pan (9 x 13 in.) with nonstick baking parchment.

2 Pour the milk into a heavy-based pan and whisk in the semolina. Bring to a boil, then simmer, stirring continuously with a wooden spoon, for 3–4 minutes or until very thick. Remove from heat and stir in the butter and cheddar cheese until melted. Whisk in the egg yolks and season to taste with salt and pepper. Pour into the lined jelly roll pan. Cover and leave to cool for 1 hour.

3 Cook the baby spinach in batches in a large pan with 1 teaspoon of water for 3–4 minutes or until wilted. Drain thoroughly and season to taste with salt, pepper, and nutmeg, then leave to cool.

4 Spread the spinach over the cooled semolina mixture and sprinkle ¾ cup of the mozzarella and half the Parmesan cheese on top. Bake in the preheated oven for 20 minutes or until golden.

5 Leave to cool, then roll up like a jelly roll. Sprinkle with the remaining mozzarella and Parmesan cheese, then bake for another 15–20 minutes or until golden. Serve immediately with freshly made tomato sauce.

INGREDIENTS
Serves 8

2 ½ cups milk
⅔ cup fine semolina or polenta
2 tbsp. butter
¾ cup grated cheddar cheese
2 medium egg yolks
salt and freshly ground black pepper
1½ lbs. baby spinach leaves
½ tsp. freshly grated nutmeg
1 ¼ cups grated mozzarella cheese
2 tbsp. freshly grated Parmesan cheese
freshly made tomato sauce, to serve

Helpful Hint

It is important to use the correct size of pan for this dish, so that the polenta mixture is thin enough to roll up. Do not be tempted to put it in the refrigerator to cool, or it will become too hard and crack when rolled.

Penne with Mixed Bell Peppers & Garlic

1 Preheat the broiler and line the broiler rack with foil. Cut the bell peppers in half, then deseed and place cut side down on the broiler rack. Cook under the broiler until the skins become blistered and black all over. Place the bell peppers in a plastic bag and let cool, then discard the skin and slice thinly.

2 Heat the olive oil in a heavy-based pan. Add the onion, celery, garlic, and bacon and cook for 4–5 minutes or until the onion has softened. Add the bell peppers and cook for 1 minute. Pour in the chicken stock and season to taste with salt and pepper. Cover and simmer for about 20 minutes.

3 Meanwhile, bring a large pan of lightly salted water to a rolling boil. Add the penne and cook according to the package directions, about 3–4 minutes or until al dente. Drain thoroughly and return to the pan.

4 Pour the bell pepper sauce over the pasta and toss lightly. Spoon into a warmed serving dish and sprinkle with the chopped parsley and grated pecorino cheese. Serve immediately with a green salad and warm whole-wheat bread.

INGREDIENTS
Serves 4

1 lb. green, red, and yellow bell peppers
2 tbsp. olive oil
1 large onion, peeled and sliced
1 celery stalk, trimmed and finely chopped
2 garlic cloves, peeled and crushed
4 slices smoked bacon, finely chopped
1¼ cups chicken stock
salt and freshly ground black pepper
3 cups fresh penne
2 tbsp. freshly chopped parsley
2 tbsp. finely grated pecorino cheese

TO SERVE:
green salad
warm whole-wheat bread

Helpful Hint

Broiling brings out all the delicious flavor of bell peppers. Make sure that they are blackened and blistered so that the skins simply slip off. You could also roast the bell peppers in the oven, if preferred. Place them in a roasting pan, then brush with a little olive oil and cook at 400° F for 25 minutes or until the skins are slightly charred.

Angel-Hair Pasta with Smoked Salmon & Jumbo Shrimp

1 Cook the baby spinach leaves in a large pan with 1 teaspoon of water for 3–4 minutes or until wilted. Drain thoroughly, then season to taste with salt, pepper, and nutmeg, and keep warm. Remove the shells from all but four of the jumbo shrimp and set aside.

2 Bring a large pan of lightly salted water to a rolling boil. Add the pasta and cook according to the package directions, about 3–4 minutes or until al dente. Drain thoroughly and return to the pan. Stir in the butter and the shelled shrimp, then cover and keep warm.

3 Beat the eggs with the dill and season well, then stir into the spaghetti and shrimp. Return the pan to the heat briefly, just long enough to lightly scramble the eggs, then remove from the heat. Carefully mix in the smoked salmon strips and the cooked spinach. Toss gently to mix. Tip into a warmed serving dish and garnish with the shrimp and dill sprigs. Serve immediately with grated Parmesan cheese.

INGREDIENTS
Serves 4

8 oz. baby spinach leaves
salt and freshly ground black pepper
pinch of freshly grated nutmeg
8 oz. cooked jumbo shrimp in their shells
1 lb. fresh angel-hair pasta
½ stick butter
3 medium eggs
1 tbsp. freshly chopped dill, plus extra to garnish
4 oz. smoked salmon, cut into strips
dill sprigs, to garnish
2 tbsp. grated Parmesan cheese, to serve

Helpful Hint

Make sure that you use cooked and not raw jumbo shrimp for this dish. If you buy them raw, remove the heads and shells, then briefly sauté in a little olive oil until just pink and opaque. This will take only 3–4 minutes; take care not to overcook them or they will toughen.

Pasta Ring with Chicken & Sun-Dried Tomatoes

1 Preheat the oven to 375° F. Lightly brush an 8-inch ring mold with a little melted butter and dust with the bread crumbs.

2 Melt ½ stick of the butter in a heavy-based pan. Add the flour and cook for 1 minute. Whisk in the milk and cook, stirring until thickened. Add the chopped onion, season with salt and pepper, and set aside.

3 Bring a large pan of lightly salted water to a rolling boil. Add the tagliatelle and cook according to the package directions, about 3–4 minutes or until al dente. Drain thoroughly and stir into the white sauce. Pour the pasta mixture into the prepared mold and bake in the preheated oven for 25–30 minutes.

4 Melt the remaining butter in a skillet, then add the chicken and cook for 4–5 minutes or until cooked. Pour in the wine and cook over a high heat for 30 seconds. Blend the cornstarch with 1 teaspoon of water and stir into the pan. Add 1 tablespoon chopped tarragon and the tomatoes. Season well, then cook for a few minutes until thickened.

5 Allow the pasta to cool for 5 minutes, then unmold onto a large plate. Fill the center with the chicken sauce. Garnish with the remaining tarragon and serve immediately.

INGREDIENTS
Serves 6

1 stick butter, plus extra for brushing

2 tbsp. natural white bread crumbs

3 tbsp. flour

about 1¼ cups milk

1 small onion, peeled and very finely chopped

salt and freshly ground black pepper

8 oz. fresh tagliatelle

1 lb. chicken breast fillets, skinned and cut into strips

¾ cup white wine

1 tsp. cornstarch

2 tbsp. freshly chopped tarragon

2 tbsp. chopped sun-dried tomatoes

Helpful Hint

To ensure that the pasta turns out easily, brush the ring mold with melted butter, then put in the freezer for 3–4 minutes to harden. Brush again with butter before dusting with the bread crumbs, making sure it is well coated.

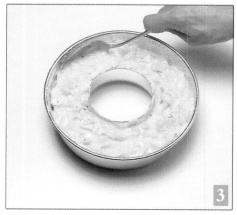

Salmon & Mushroom Linguine

1 Preheat the oven to 375° F. Place the salmon in a shallow pan and cover with water. Season well with salt and pepper and bring to a boil, then lower the heat and simmer for 6–8 minutes or until cooked. Drain and keep warm.

2 Melt ½ stick of the butter in a heavy-based pan. Stir in the flour and cook for 1 minute, then whisk in the chicken stock. Simmer gently until thickened. Stir in the cream and season to taste with salt and pepper. Keep the sauce warm.

3 Melt the remaining butter in a pan, then add the sliced mushrooms and cook for 2–3 minutes. Stir the mushrooms into the white sauce.

4 Bring a large pan of lightly salted water to a rolling boil. Add the linguine and cook according to the package directions or until al dente.

5 Drain the pasta thoroughly and return to the pan. Stir in half the sauce, then spoon into a lightly greased, 1¼-quart, shallow ovenproof dish. Flake the salmon and add to the remaining sauce, then pour over the pasta. Sprinkle with the cheese and bread crumbs, then bake in the preheated oven for 15–20 minutes or until golden. Garnish with the parsley and serve immediately.

INGREDIENTS
Serves 4

1 lb. salmon fillets, skinned
salt and freshly ground black
  pepper
¾ stick butter
3 tbsp. flour
1¼ cups chicken stock
⅔ cup whipping cream
2½ cups mushrooms, wiped and
  sliced
12 oz. linguine
½ cup grated cheddar cheese
1 cup fresh white bread crumbs
2 tbsp. freshly chopped parsley,
  to garnish

Helpful Hint

When cooking the salmon, the poaching liquid should be just simmering and not boiling rapidly. Add extra flavor if you like by putting in a bay leaf and a sprig of fresh thyme or a thinly pared strip of lemon rind. The salmon should be slightly undercooked in this recipe, as it will then be baked in the oven.

Spaghetti with Hot Chili Mussels

1 Scrub the mussels and remove any beards. Discard any that do not close when tapped. Place in a large pan with the white wine and half the crushed garlic. Cover and cook over a high heat for 5 minutes, shaking the pan from time to time. When the mussels have opened, drain, setting aside the juices and straining them through a cheesecloth-lined sieve. Discard any mussels that have not opened and keep the rest warm.

2 Heat the oil in a heavy-based pan, then add the remaining garlic with the chilies and cook for about 30 seconds. Stir in the chopped tomatoes and ⅓ cup of the cooking liquid

and simmer for 15–20 minutes. Season to taste with salt and pepper.

3 Meanwhile, bring a large pan of lightly salted water to a rolling boil. Add the spaghetti and cook according to the package directions, about 3–4 minutes or until al dente.

4 Drain the spaghetti thoroughly and return to the pan. Add the mussels and tomato sauce to the pasta and toss lightly to cover, then spoon into a warmed serving dish or onto individual plates. Garnish with chopped parsley and serve immediately with warm crusty bread.

INGREDIENTS
Serves 4

2 lb. fresh live mussels
1¼ cups white wine
3–4 garlic cloves, peeled and crushed
2 tbsp. olive oil
1–2 bird's eye chilies, deseeded and chopped
2 14-oz. cans chopped tomatoes
salt and freshly ground black pepper
12 oz. fresh spaghetti
2 tbsp. freshly chopped parsley, to garnish
warm, crusty bread, to serve

Food Fact

Mussels are bivalves (which means they have two shells hinged together) with blue-black colored shells. They attach themselves to rocks on the seabed and take up to two years to mature. They are usually sold in netted bags, either by weight or volume. If you buy by volume, you will need 1 quart for this recipe.

Conchiglioni with Crab au Gratin

1 Preheat the oven to 400° F. Bring a large pan of lightly salted water to a rolling boil. Add the pasta shells and cook according to the package directions or until al dente. Drain the pasta thoroughly and allow it to dry completely.

2 Melt half the butter in a heavy-based pan. Add the shallots and chili, and cook for 2 minutes, then stir in the crabmeat. Stuff the cooled shells with the crab mixture and set aside.

3 Melt the remaining butter in a small pan and stir in the flour. Cook for about 1 minute, then whisk in the wine and milk and cook, stirring until thickened. Stir in the crème fraîche and grated cheese and season with salt and pepper.

4 Place the crab-filled shells in a lightly greased, large, shallow baking dish or tray, and spoon a little of the sauce on top. Toss the bread crumbs in the melted butter or oil, then sprinkle over the pasta shells. Bake in the preheated oven for 10 minutes. Serve immediately with a cheese or tomato sauce and a tossed green salad or cooked baby vegetables.

INGREDIENTS
Serves 4

6 oz. large pasta shells
½ stick butter
1 shallot, peeled and finely chopped
1 bird's eye chili, deseeded and finely chopped
2 7-oz. cans crabmeat, drained
3 tbsp. all-purpose flour
¼ cup white wine
¼ cup milk
3 tbsp. crème fraîche
1½ tbsp. grated cheddar cheese
salt and freshly ground black pepper
1 tbsp. oil or melted butter
1 cup fresh white bread crumbs

TO SERVE:

cheese or tomato sauce
tossed green salad or freshly cooked baby vegetables

Helpful Hint

Canned crabmeat is preserved in brine, so drain well and do not add too much salt when seasoning. Crab is in season between April and December and is least expensive during these months, so consider buying fresh white crabmeat for this recipe; you will need a medium-sized crab that weighs about 12 oz.

Pappardelle with Spicy Lamb & Bell Peppers

1 Preheat the broiler just before cooking. Fry the ground lamb in a skillet until browned. Heat the olive oil in a heavy-based pan, then add the onion, garlic, and all the chopped bell peppers and cook gently for 3–4 minutes or until softened. Add the browned ground lamb to the pan and cook, stirring, until the onions have softened, then drain off any remaining oil.

2 Stir the chili powder and cumin into the pan and cook gently for 2 minutes. Add the tomato paste, then pour in the wine and season to taste with salt and pepper. Reduce the heat and simmer for 10–15 minutes or until the sauce has reduced.

3 Meanwhile, bring a large pan of lightly salted water to a rolling boil. Add the papardelle and cook according to the package directions or until al dente. Drain thoroughly, then return to the pan and stir the meat sauce into the pasta. Keep warm.

4 Meanwhile, place the bread crumbs on a cookie sheet, drizzle the melted butter over the bread crumbs, and place under the preheated broiler for 3–4 minutes or until golden and crispy. Let cool, then mix with the grated cheddar cheese. Spoon the pasta mixture into a warmed serving dish, then sprinkle with the bread crumbs and parsley. Serve immediately.

INGREDIENTS
Serves 4

1 lb. fresh ground lamb
2 tbsp. olive oil
1 onion, peeled and finely chopped
2 garlic cloves, peeled and crushed
1 green bell pepper, deseeded and chopped
1 yellow bell pepper, deseeded and chopped
½ tsp. hot chili powder
1 tsp. ground cumin
1 tbsp. tomato paste
⅔ cup red wine
salt and freshly ground black pepper
12 oz. pappardelle
1 cup fresh white bread crumbs
2 tbsp. butter, melted
¼ cup grated cheddar cheese
1 tbsp. freshly chopped parsley

Tasty Tip

Choose very lean ground lamb for this dish. To add extra flavor, add a fresh bay leaf or a sprig of fresh rosemary to the pan when frying the ground lamb and remove at the end of step 2, when the sauce has reduced.

Farfalle with Zucchini & Mushrooms

1 Heat the butter and olive oil in a large pan. Add the onion, garlic, and bacon lardons, and cook for 3–4 minutes or until the onion has softened. Add the zucchini and cook, stirring, for 3–4 minutes. Add the mushrooms, then lower the heat and cook covered for 4–5 minutes.

2 Meanwhile, bring a large pan of lightly salted water to a rolling boil. Add the farfalle and cook according to the package directions or until al dente. Drain thoroughly, then return to the pan and keep warm.

3 Season the mushroom mixture to taste, then stir in the crème fraîche and half the chopped parsley. Simmer for 2–3 minutes or until the sauce is thick and creamy.

4 Pour the sauce over the cooked pasta. Toss lightly, then reheat for 2 minutes or until piping hot. Spoon into a warmed serving dish and sprinkle over the chopped parsley. Garnish with pecorino cheese shavings and serve immediately with mixed salad leaves and crusty bread.

INGREDIENTS
Serves 4

2 tbsp. butter
2 tsp. olive oil
1 small onion, peeled and finely chopped
2 garlic cloves, peeled and crushed
scant ½ cup bacon lardons
2½ cups zucchini, trimmed and diced
2 cups button mushrooms, wiped and roughly chopped
3 cups farfalle
salt and freshly ground black pepper
1 cup crème fraîche
2 tbsp. freshly chopped parsley
shaved pecorino cheese, to garnish

TO SERVE:
mixed salad leaves
crusty bread

Helpful Hint

To shave pecorino or Parmesan cheese, use a sharp knife or a vegetable peeler. If you find this difficult, you could coarsely grate the cheese instead. Avoid tubs of ready-grated pecorino and Parmesan; they tend to be powdery and flavorless, and are a poor substitute for fresh cheese.

Cannelloni with Tomato & Red Wine Sauce

1 Preheat the oven to 400° F. Heat the oil in a heavy-based pan, then add the onion and garlic and cook for 2–3 minutes. Cool slightly, then stir in the ricotta cheese and pine nuts. Season the filling to taste with salt, pepper, and the nutmeg.

2 Cut each lasagna sheet in half. Put a little of the ricotta filling on each piece and roll up like a cigar to resemble cannelloni tubes. Arrange the cannelloni, seam-side down, in a single layer, in a lightly greased, 2-quart shallow oven-proof dish.

3 Melt the butter in a pan, then add the shallot and cook for 2 minutes. Pour in the red wine, tomatoes, and sugar and season well. Bring to a boil, then lower the heat and simmer for about 20 minutes or until thickened. Add a little more sugar if desired. Transfer to a food processor and blend until a smooth sauce is formed.

4 Pour the warm tomato sauce over the cannelloni and sprinkle with the grated mozzarella cheese. Bake in the preheated oven for about 30 minutes or until golden and bubbling. Garnish and serve immediately with a green salad.

INGREDIENTS
Serves 6

2 tbsp. olive oil
1 onion, peeled and finely chopped
1 garlic clove, peeled and crushed
1 cup ricotta cheese
scant ⅓ cup pine nuts
salt and freshly ground black pepper
pinch freshly grated nutmeg
9 oz. fresh spinach lasagna
2 tbsp. butter
1 shallot, peeled and finely chopped
⅔ cup red wine
2 14-oz. cans chopped tomatoes
½ tsp. sugar
½ cup grated mozzarella cheese, plus extra to serve
1 tbsp. freshly chopped parsley, to garnish
fresh green salad, to serve

Food Fact

Mozzarella is the Italian cheese often used to top pizzas, as it is elastic and stringy when cooked. It is a soft, kneaded, brilliantly white cheese with a delicate, almost spongy texture. Traditionally, it was made from buffalo milk, but now cow's milk is more often used.

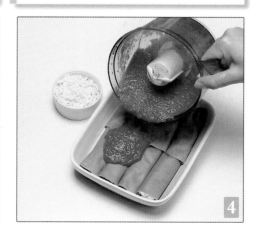

Pasta Triangles with Pesto & Walnut Dressing

1 Preheat the broiler to high. Cut the lasagna sheets in half, then into triangles, and set aside. Mix the pesto and ricotta cheese together, and warm gently in a pan.

2 Toast the walnuts under the preheated broiler until golden. Rub off the skins. Place the nuts in a food processor with the bread and grind finely.

3 Mix the sour cream with the mascarpone cheese in a bowl. Add the ground walnuts and pecorino cheese, and season to taste with salt and pepper. Whisk in the olive oil. Pour into a pan and warm gently.

4 Bring a large pan of lightly salted water to a rolling boil. Add the pasta triangles and cook, according to the package directions, about 3–4 minutes or until al dente.

5 Drain the pasta thoroughly and arrange a few triangles on each serving plate. Top each one with a spoonful of the pesto mixture, then place another triangle on top. Continue to layer the pasta and pesto mixture, then spoon a little of the walnut sauce on top of each stack. Garnish with dill, basil, or parsley, and serve immediately with a freshly dressed tomato and cucumber salad.

INGREDIENTS
Serves 6

1 lb. fresh egg lasagna
4 tbsp. pesto
4 tbsp. ricotta cheese
1 cup shelled walnuts
1 slice white bread, crusts removed
⅔ cup sour cream
⅓ cup mascarpone cheese
¼ cup grated pecorino cheese
salt and freshly ground black pepper
1 tbsp. olive oil
sprig of dill or freshly chopped basil or parsley, to garnish
tomato and cucumber salad, to serve

Tasty Tip

For a simple tomato and cucumber salad, arrange overlapping thin slices of cucumbers and tomatoes on a large plate. Drizzle on top a dressing made with 1 teaspoon Dijon mustard, 4 tablespoons extra-virgin olive oil, 1 tablespoon lemon juice, and a pinch each of sugar, salt, and pepper. Leave at room temperature for 15 minutes before serving.

Eggplant & Tomato Layer

1 Preheat the oven to 375° F. Brush the eggplant slices with 5 tablespoons of the olive oil and place on a cookie sheet. Bake in the preheated oven for 20 minutes or until tender. Remove from the oven and increase the temperature to 400° F.

2 Heat the remaining oil in a heavy-based pan. Add the onion and garlic. Cook for 2–3 minutes, then add the tomatoes, wine, and sugar. Season to taste with salt and pepper, then simmer for 20 minutes.

3 Melt the butter in another pan. Stir in the flour and cook for 2 minutes, then whisk in the milk. Cook for 2–3 minutes or until thickened. Season to taste.

4 Pour a little white sauce into a lightly greased baking dish. Cover with a layer of lasagna and spread with tomato sauce, then add some of the eggplant. Cover thinly with white sauce and sprinkle with a little mozzarella cheese. Continue to layer in this way, finishing with a layer of lasagna.

5 Beat together the eggs and yogurt. Season, then pour over the lasagna. Sprinkle with the remaining cheese and bake in the preheated oven for 25–30 minutes or until golden. Garnish with basil leaves and serve.

INGREDIENTS
Serves 4

2 eggplants, about 1½ lb., trimmed
  and thinly sliced
6 tbsp. olive oil
1 onion, peeled and finely sliced
1 garlic clove, peeled and crushed
14-oz. can chopped tomatoes
¼ cup red wine
½ tsp. sugar
salt and freshly ground black
  pepper
½ stick butter
3 tbsp. flour
1¾ cups milk
8 oz. fresh egg lasagna
2 medium eggs, beaten
¾ cup plain yogurt
1¼ cups grated mozzarella cheese
fresh basil leaves, to garnish

Food Fact

Technically a fruit, but generally classified as a vegetable, eggplants originated in India. Eggplants are now grown throughout the world, and are widely used in a variety of regional cuisines.

Cannelloni with Gorgonzola Sauce

1 Preheat the oven to 375° F. Melt the salted butter in a heavy-based pan, then add the shallot and bacon, and cook for about 4–5 minutes.

2 Add the mushrooms to the pan and cook for 5–6 minutes or until the mushrooms are very soft. Stir in the flour and cook for 1 minute, then stir in the heavy cream and cook gently for an additional 2 minutes. Let cool.

3 Cut each sheet of lasagna in half. Spoon some filling onto each piece and roll up from the longest side to resemble cannelloni. Arrange the cannelloni in a lightly greased, shallow 1¼-quart ovenproof dish.

4 Heat the unsalted butter very slowly in a pan, and when it is melted, add the Gorgonzola cheese. Stir until the cheese has melted, then stir in the whipping cream. Bring to a boil slowly, then simmer gently for about 5 minutes or until thickened.

5 Pour the cream sauce over the cannelloni. Place in the preheated oven and bake for 20 minutes or until golden and completely heated through. Serve immediately with assorted salad leaves.

INGREDIENTS
Serves 2–3

½ stick salted butter

1 shallot, peeled and finely chopped

2 slices bacon, rind removed and chopped

4 cups wiped and finely chopped mushrooms

2 tbsp. all-purpose flour

½ cup heavy cream

4 oz. fresh egg lasagna, 6 sheets in total

3 tbsp. unsalted butter

1¼ cups diced Gorgonzola cheese

⅔ cup whipping cream

assorted lettuce leaves, to serve

Tasty Tip

Gorgonzola cheese is very salty. As it is combined in this recipe with bacon, which is also salty, some of the butter used here is unsalted in order to balance the flavor. Italians use a wide range of mushrooms in their cooking, so for extra taste, you could use chestnut or large open-field mushrooms instead of ordinary button mushrooms.

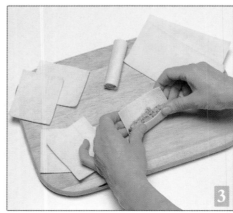

Ratatouille & Pasta Bake

1 Preheat the oven to 375° F. Heat the olive oil in a heavy-based pan, then add half the onion and cook gently for 2–3 minutes. Stir in the tomatoes and wine, then simmer for 20 minutes or until a thick consistency is formed. Add the sugar and season to taste with salt and pepper. Set aside.

2 Meanwhile, melt the butter in another pan, then add the remaining onion, the garlic, mushrooms, and zucchini, and cook for 10 minutes or until softened.

3 Spread a little tomato sauce in the base of a lightly greased baking dish. Top with a layer of lasagna and spoon over half the mushroom and zucchini mixture. Repeat the layers, finishing with a layer of lasagna.

4 Beat the eggs and cream together, then pour over the lasagna. Mix the mozzarella and pecorino cheeses together, then sprinkle on top of the lasagna. Place in the preheated oven and cook for about 20 minutes or until golden brown. Serve immediately with a green salad.

INGREDIENTS
Serves 4

1 tbsp. olive oil
2 large onions, peeled and finely chopped
14-oz. can chopped tomatoes
7 tbsp. white wine
½ tsp. sugar
salt and freshly ground black pepper
3 tbsp. butter
2 garlic cloves, peeled and crushed
2 cups mushrooms, wiped and thickly sliced
1½ lbs. zucchini, trimmed and thickly sliced
4 oz. fresh spinach lasagna
2 large eggs
2 tbsp. heavy cream
¾ cup grated mozzarella cheese
¼ cup grated pecorino cheese
green salad, to serve

Tasty Tip

For speed and simplicity, this recipe is a simplified version of ratatouille. If preferred, it can be made more traditionally by substituting a small chopped eggplant and a deseeded and chopped green or red bell pepper for some of the zucchini.

Lamb & Pasta Pie

1 Preheat the oven to 375° F. Lightly grease an 8-inch spring-form cake pan. Blend the flour, salt, margarine, and white vegetable fat in a food processor and add sufficient cold water to make a smooth, pliable dough. Knead on a lightly floured surface, then roll out two thirds to line the base and sides of the tin. Brush the pastry with egg white and set aside.

2 Melt the butter in a heavy-based pan, stir in the flour, and cook for 2 minutes. Stir in the milk and cook, stirring, until a smooth, thick sauce is formed. Season to taste with salt and pepper and set aside.

3 Bring a large pan of lightly salted water to a rolling boil. Add the macaroni and cook according to the package directions or until al dente. Drain, then stir into the white sauce with the grated cheese.

4 Heat the oil in a skillet. Add the onion, garlic, celery, and ground lamb and cook, stirring, for 5–6 minutes. Stir in the tomato paste and tomatoes and cook for 10 minutes. Cool slightly.

5 Place half the pasta mixture, then all the ground lamb in the pastry-lined tin. Top with a layer of pasta. Roll out the remaining pastry and cut out a lid. Brush the edge with water, then place over the filling and pinch the edges together. Use trimmings to decorate the top.

6 Brush the pie with beaten egg yolk and bake in the preheated oven for 50–60 minutes; cover the top with tin foil if it browns too quickly. Stand for 15 minutes before turning out. Serve immediately.

INGREDIENTS
Serves 8

2⅔ cup all-purpose flour
about ½ cup margarine
about ½ cup vegetable shortening
pinch of salt
1 small egg, separated
½ stick butter
⅓ cup flour
1¾ cups milk
salt and freshly ground black pepper
2 cups macaroni
½ cup grated cheddar cheese
1 tbsp. vegetable oil
1 onion, peeled and chopped
1 garlic clove, peeled and crushed
2 celery stalks, trimmed and chopped
1 lb. ground lamb
1 tbsp. tomato paste
14-oz. can chopped tomatoes

Baked Macaroni with Mushrooms & Leeks

1 Preheat the oven to 425° F. Heat 1 tablespoon of the olive oil in a large skillet, then add the onion and garlic and cook for 2 minutes. Add the leeks, mushrooms, and 2 tablespoons of the butter, then cook for 5 minutes. Pour in the white wine and cook for 2 minutes, then stir in the crème fraîche or cream. Season to taste with salt and pepper.

2 Meanwhile, bring a large pan of lightly salted water to a rolling boil. Add the macaroni and cook according to the package directions or until al dente.

3 Melt 2 tablespoons of the butter with the remaining oil in a small skillet. Add the bread crumbs and fry until just beginning to turn golden brown. Drain on paper towels.

4 Drain the pasta thoroughly. Toss in the remaining butter, then spoon into a lightly greased shallow baking dish. Cover the pasta with the leek and mushroom mixture, then sprinkle with the fried bread crumbs. Bake in the preheated oven for 5–10 minutes or until golden and crisp. Garnish with chopped parsley and serve.

INGREDIENTS
Serves 4

2 tbsp. olive oil
1 onion, peeled and finely chopped
1 garlic clove, peeled and crushed
2 small leeks, trimmed and chopped
1 lb. assorted wild mushrooms, trimmed
¾ stick butter
¼ cup white wine
⅔ cup crème fraîche or whipping cream
salt and freshly ground black pepper
3 cups short-cut macaroni
1½ cups fresh white bread crumbs
1 tbsp. freshly chopped parsley, to garnish

Helpful Hint

Some wild mushrooms are more tender and cook faster than others. Chestnut, porcini, portabella, enoki, and shiitake would all be good for this recipe. If you use chanterelles or oyster mushrooms, sauté them with the leeks for 1 minute only, as they are fairly delicate.

INDEX